The Unauthorized Trek

THE COMPLETE

NEXT GENERATION

James Van Hise
Hal Schuster

PIONEER BOOKS INC

Recently Released Pioneer Books...

Library of Congress Cataloging-in-Publication Data
James Van Hise, 1959—
Hal Schuster, 1955—

   The Unauthorized Trek: The Complete Next Generation

   1.   The Unauthorized Trek: The Complete Next Generation

           (television, popular culture)
 I. Title

Published by Pioneer Books, Inc., 5715 N. Balsam Rd., Las Vegas, NV, 89130.

First Printing, 1995

PUBLISHER, EDITOR, DESIGNER: Hal Schuster
COVER ART BY Bruce Wood, COVER DESIGN BY Hal Schuster
All photos Copyright ©1995 Albert L. Ortega.

TABLE OF CONTENTS

The Unauthorized Trek

THE COMPLETE

GUIDE TO
THE NEXT GENERATION

I've already written many guides to THE NEXT GENERATION, so the question arises: "Why write another one?" This one differs completely from any earlier work. As they say, it is all new and greatly improved. It covers all 178 episodes of STAR TREK: THE NEXT GENERATION in very complete reviews.

Stronger analysis adds much to the work. Descriptions of scenes appear only to poke beneath the surface and avoid the ordinary approach to an episode guide. James Van Hise wrote most reviews, while Wendy Rathbone, co-author of the UNOFFICIAL TREK: THE ENCYCLOPEDIA, added many of her own contributions. Hal Schuster rewrote the draft manuscript and added some comments of his own. These are identified where they appear. She gave her own different insights into episodes also reviewed by Van Hise. They combine to offer a fascinating dual perspective. Hal Schuster added his own words throughout the book.

In other words: it's unique, it's different, and it's fun.

SEASON

ONE

STAR TREK went back to the drawing board. Anything was possible. Would it rise to new highs or sink to new lows in the universe created by Gene Roddenberry. The truth fell somewhere in-between for the first season.

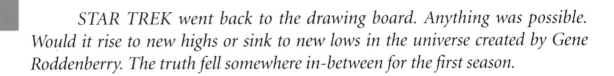

SEASON ONE

EPISODES ONE AND TWO: "ENCOUNTER AT FARPOINT"
Written by D.C. Fontana and Gene Roddenberry
Directed by Corey Allen
Guest Cast: John deLancie, Michael Bell, DeForest Kelley, Colm Meaney, Cary Hiroyuki, Timothy Dang, David Erskine, Evelyn Guerrero, Chuck Hicks

This story started it all. Fans still argue about it. Its structure is weaker than that of other two-part episodes in the series because it started as two different stories.

The story introduces the new Enterprise and its crew as they meet Q. After a prolonged remake of incidents from the original STAR TREK episode "Squire of Gothos," the new story sends the Enterprise to Starpoint station where they detect a mystery. Dorothy (D.C.) Fontana wrote the "Farpoint" segments while Roddenberry wrote the "Q" parts. Then Roddenberry combined the two in an uneasy mix.

Q closely resembles Trelane, from "Squire of Gothos."Everyone except Roddenberry noticed this. Roddenberry was notorious for forgetting his past work. He never seemed to noice that STAR TREK: THE MOTION PICTURE closely resembles the original STAR TREK episode, "The Changeling."

Q is a remarkably annoying but uninteresting character. Roddenberry's fascination with him seems inexplicable until the second season episode, "Q Who," when he is better written. John de Lancie's portrayal of Q changes in that later episode as Q becomes much less like Trelane. They almost hired William Campbell to reprise his Trelane character and meet Q. The only initial difference between the characters was that while Trelane was an alien child, Q only acted like an alien child.

Even before I knew the tale of the scripting of "Encounter At Farpoint," I was uncomfortable with the story. One storyline has nothing to do with the other. Roddenberry seemed to have forgotten how to tell a good story. Many first season episodes offered dual, and dueling, storylines. Parallel plots clashed with nothing to connect them. Roddenberry consistently offered one plot with the Enterprise in jeopardy, and another with the main characters in separate danger on a planet.

This episode also established an unfortunate tradition only fixed much later. Picard surrenders in the heat of battle. Captain Kirk *never* surrendered in the original series. He would have died first and taken the ship with him. When Kirk surrenders in STAR TREK VI: THE UNDISCOVERED COUNTRY, it's a shock because he'd never done it before! Having Picard surrender in the very first episode weakened the character.

It forced an unfavorable comparison with Kirk. It also underscored the weakness of having families aboard the Enterprise. Danger threatens not only Starfleet personnel, an accepted part of the job, but innocent civilians, including young children. Writers found this an uncomfortable proposition. Entire seasons passed without mentioning the civilians on the Enterprise.

This episode featured a saucer separation. Two halves of the Enterprise went their separate ways. Roddenberry originally wanted to do this in STAR TREK: THE MOTION PICTURE but was stopped by time constraints on the shooting schedule.

The portrayal of giant alien life forms maintained Roddenberry's idea that non-humans possessed the same rights as humans. The lovely conclusion almost succeeded in balancing the sins in the story. Viewers remember the ending better than what came before.

EPISODE THREE: "THE NAKED NOW"

Teleplay by J. Michael Bingham
Story by John D.F. Black and J. Michael Bingham
Directed by Paul Lynch
Guest Cast: Benjamin W.S. Lum, Michael Rider, David Renan, Skip Stellrecht, Kenny Koch

"The Naked Time" was the name of an early episode of the original STAR TREK. NEXT GENERATION offered "The Naked Now" as a sequel. It failed to capture the best elements of the original. "The Naked Time" offered humorous scenes but concentrated on drama. A strange virus brings the subconscious feelings and desires of the crew to the surface. One commits suicide in front of his shipmates. Nothing that dramatic occurs in "The Naked Now."

The new story retains the idea of the Enterprise trapped in orbit around an unstable celestial body, but the rest is low key. Tasha Yar seduces Data in the most unusual scene in the episode. "The Naked Time" used dramatic events to reveal the crew while "The Naked Now" told little about the characters. They act silly instead of honest.

John D.F. Black worked on both episodes. He was not given a free hand on NEXT GENERATION, and never wrote for the series again. It apparently wasn't a very rewarding writing experience. The remake forces another unfortunate comparison with the original STAR TREK series.

Removing inhibitions from characters in "The Naked Time" reveals private demons, deepening the portrayals. "The Naked Now" fails to deliver this; strange actions merely appear strange.

EPISODE FOUR: "CODE OF HONOR"

Teleplay by Kathryn Powers and Michael Baron
Directed by Russ Mayberry

Guest Cast: Jessie Lawrence Ferguson, Karole Selmon, James Louis Watkins, Michael Rider

The attempt to save money appears on screen. Roddenberry reportedly cast black actors instead of using makeup to portray aliens. They wore costumes seemingly taken right off the rack from a wardrobe formerly used in an Arabian Nights epic.

The episode offers an interesting culture wherein women control and inherit all property, but it's never developed beyond what is required for the climax. Such cultures exist in our current world.

The world ruler kidnaps Tasha Yar for his collection of wives. Picard again appears impotent. Federation policy prevents his taking aggressive action after his officer has been kidnapped. Starfleet appears weak and ineffectual, speaking loudly but carrying no stick. The fault lies with the script. Had Picard stressed Federation protocol as being as important as the Ligonians, grounds for respect would have been established.

The Ligonians take great enjoyment in challenging a strong foe and watching them squirm. The climax takes elements from "Amok Time" when a combatant dies and is later revived on the Enterprise.

This story needs rewrites.

EPISODE FIVE: "THE LAST OUTPOST"

Teleplay by Herbert Wright
Story by Richard Krzemian
Directed by Richard Colla
Guest Cast: Darryl Henriques, Mike Gomez, Armin Shimerman, Jake Dengal, Tracey Walter

This episode introduced the Ferengi. It sends a mixed message. Ugly, vicious Ferengi attack an away team with stinging electric whips, but appear laughable as five foot tall villains. A throwaway line in an earlier episode revealed that even Klingons are afraid of Ferengi. Any Klingon afraid of a Ferengi would commit suicide out of shame and dishonor.

They borrowed the plot from the original STAR TREK episode, "Arena." A superior alien intelligence observes the Enterprise and the Ferengi vessel bent on combat and renders them helpless. He wants to learn about the crews, and the nature of the true aggressor. Just as Captain Kirk refused to destroy the Gorn when he triumphed, Will Riker turns down the offer to kill the Ferengi.

The only interesting line appears when the Ferengi see Tasha Yar. They remark how disgusting it is that humans make their females wear clothing. Sounds like a Roddenberry line to me.

Armin Shimmerman appears as a Ferengi. Years later he stepped back into those shoes to play Quark on DEEP SPACE NINE. By that time any Ferengi menace had been completely emasculated. The ruthless merchants lack individuality. Their culture brainwashes them into acting and thinking alike, with little deviation from the norm. Ferengi rarely rise above the level of cartoon characters.

The dead planet in this episode contains the remnants of an ancient civilization, but it is never explored. Another "Enterprise in jeopardy" subplot fills time instead. THE NEXT GENERATION got off to a slow start. Nothing in early episodes suggested how good the series would become.

EPISODE SIX: "WHERE NO ONE HAS GONE BEFORE"
Written by Diane Duane and Michael Reaves
Directed by Rob Bowman
Guest Cast: Biff Yeager, Charles Dayton, Victoria Dillard, Stanley Kamel, Eric Menyuk, Herta Ware

NEXT GENERATION finally did something STAR TREK hadn't done before. It was reason to celebrate.

No silly subplots put the Enterprise in jeopardy. They left that to the main plot.

Eric Menyuk played the alien called The Traveler in a provocative performance. Menyuk perfectly underplayed his character, hinting at mystery left unspoken, leaving us gasping for more. Menyuk had tested for the role of Data.

The Enterprise goes beyond the known galaxy, ergo the title. It captures the sense of wonder only science fiction can achieve, something television rarely tries.

This is a Wesley Crusher episode, but it isn't annoying. The character shows some dignity. Too many early episodes posed Wesley grinning for the camera like a little kid instead of a 16 year old. This episode gave Wesley Crusher stature. The excellent story appears to be a first season fluke. Ideas introduced were ultimately resolved in season seven's "Journey's End."

EPISODE SEVEN: "LONELY AMONG US"
Script by D.C. Fontana
Story by Michael Halperin
Directed by Cliff Bole
Guest Cast: Colm Meaney, Kavi Raz, John Durbin

Episode seven returned to normal, dismal standards with an unimaginative story. They lifted an idea from the original STAR TREK episode "Journey To Babel."

An Enterprise again transports alien delegations to a peace conference. The delegations hate each other. This time one race devours their enemies. Much is made of this at the beginning of the episode, but it is forgotten for the rest of the story. One wonders what purpose it served.

The episode introduced what would become a recurring plot when a disembodied entity slipped aboard the Enterprise to stir up trouble. It took over the body of one crewman after another in search of something, and finally settled in Captain Picard. When it's discovered because it makes stupid decisions, it displays great powers. Then it apologizes for all the trouble it caused and leaves! It is apparently part of a greater group mind. The Enterprise crew learn little, missing an obvious opportunity to communicate.

Dorothy Fontana wrote the script, but it has Gene Roddenberry's fingerprints all over it. The rewrite was clumsy, particularly since the feuding delegations never become part of the story or are given more than silly cartoon portrayals. Many possibilities remain unexplored.

An interesting side note occurs when a scene in the briefing room shows a model of the Galileo 7 in the background. It is the original special effects miniature of the shuttle craft used in the classic series. Greg Jein restored the model.

EPISODE EIGHT: "JUSTICE"

Teleplay by Worley Thorne
Story by Ralph Willis and Worley Thorne
Directed by James L. Conway
Guest Cast: Josh Clark, David Q. Combs, Richard Lavin, Judith Jones, Eric Matthew, Brad Zerbst, David Michael Graves

This episode displays the best and the worst of the first season. An unfortunate flaw underlies the story.

The Enterprise finds a previously unexplored Class M (Earth like) planet with an advanced civilization. Although nothing is known about their culture, Captain Picard grants his crew shore leave, and no one questions his wisdom!

Crew members mingle with scantily clad, very affectionate, young, attractive aliens. When a blond beauty gets friendly with Worf, the Klingon soberly observes, "Nice planet." It was quickly dubbed the Planet of the Joggers by fans.

An unseen serpent lies waiting in this garden of Eden. Wesley accidentally falls on a protected flower. Ignorance of the law is no excuse, and Wesley is sentenced to death. The joyful people on that planet know that if they make a mistake, the sentence is death. No one questions this as it's the way it has always been. Laws are handed down and enforced by an orbiting space station, the "god" of these people.

The Enterprise is also endangered. The "god" cuts off power in the Enterprise. As the temperature drops, everyone huddles together for warmth, but no one puts on heavy clothing! Couldn't someone have considered the obvious? Did the budget lack money for coats and mittens?

Picard's defense of Wesley, and pursuit of justice in a society that never questions Draconian laws, is heartfelt and intelligent. The aliens cannot defend their position except to say that it prevents crime and anarchy.

This potentially interesting story fails to effectively portray the alien culture. It poorly demonstrates the drastic differences in law and justice found within alien societies. It would have been more interesting if Wesley had done genuine harm, such as

Gene Roddenberry proudly took responsibility for another badly written Q episode. Q proved insufferable in the first season, disrupting the crew of the Enterprise. This episode offers two stories with Q as the pivotal point, but still barely held together.

First Q plays games with the crew, pitting them against alien creatures. When crew members die, Q revives them. Some applauded when Wesley Crusher was stabbed in the back, but the cheering proved short-lived.

Some complain that Wesley was unfairly picked on. Even Wesley's critics didn't blame actor Wil Wheaton; they blamed the writers and directors. Wesley lacked a personality in many episodes. His appearances in the early shows left him standing around grinning as if this is all kids do. He quickly became annoying.

After Wesley and the others return to the Enterprise, Q adds a new level to the game. He gives Riker the power of the Q. Riker restrains from using the power to show Q that he doesn't need it to prove his worth. He even refuses to bring a child back to life and accepts the consequences. It provides powerful emotional impact.

This scene was the exception in the first season. It's the saving grace in an otherwise bad teleplay.

Roddenberry used the climax from the classic series episode "Squire of Gothos." The original story concluded when Trelane's parents forced him to return home with them. Here other Q forcibly bring him home, admonishing him for misusing his powers.

EPISODE ELEVEN: "HAVEN"

Teleplay by Tracy Torme
Story by Tracy Torme and Lian Okun
Directed by Richard Compton
Guest Cast: Danzita Kingsley, Carel Struycken, Anna Katrina, Raye Birk, Michael Rider, Majel Barrett, Rob Knepper, Nan Martin, Robert Ellenstein

The only character fans love and hate as much as Wesley Crusher is Lwaxana Troi. Gene Roddenberry once told Majel that he'd written the perfect part for her, and she didn't even have to act. It's a wonder she didn't kill him after she read the script.

Lwaxana Troi's badly written appearances continued longer than those of Q. She only broke out of the one note character in "Half A Life." "Haven" and too many others presented Lwaxana Troi as a good-natured shrew. Majel Barrett previously played Number One in "The Cage," and Nurse Chapel for the original STAR TREK. At least the characters are all quite different.

Troi's mother comes on board because of an arranged marriage between Deanna and a young man named Wyatt, whom Deanna never met. Wyatt doesn't know what Deanna looks like but he's painted pictures of his dream girl. It's puzzling that he never asked for photos of his betrothed.

An interesting segment shows a plague ship containing the sole survivors of a colony devastated years before. There is no cure for the plague and no world will allow contact with a ship from that doomed colony. When Wyatt sees his dream woman on the allowing someone to hold a phaser and vaporize their next of kin. This examination of the conflicts of justice would have been much more fascinating. The deck is too stacked.

Interesting disagreements arise when two legitimate sides to a debate examine their ethics. This silly story offers a death sentence for walking on the grass.

EPISODE NINE: "THE BATTLE"

Teleplay by Herbert Wright
Story by Larry Forester
Directed by Rob Bowman
Guest Cast: Frank Corsentino, Doug Warhit, Robert Towers

This marked the second appearance of the Ferengi, and the introduction of the Stargazer, Picard's first command. Abandoned years before, following a battle with a mystery ship, it was believed lost until a Ferengi, Daimon Bok, returned it to Picard. The question arises why a Ferengi, one of a race of super capitalists, would give anything away free. Since profit is their only motive, it's amusing to see the astonishment when their commander presents Picard with the gift.

The Ferengi want vengeance.

The original battle won by the Stargazer was the first known contact between the Federation and the Ferengi. The Ferengi captain who died in that battle was Daimon Bok's son. An insane Bok cares not that the Ferengi ship attacked without provocation, only that Picard killed his son.

In the most interesting scene, a mentally dominated Picard relates the tale of the battle of the Stargazer and the mystery ship. They never show the battle in flashback. Don't tell us about it, show us what happened! What Picard says is more interesting than the episode.

At first Picard is happy to see the Stargazer again, but the vessel is booby trapped with a mind control device Picard must overcome. Bok altered the ship's logs to make it appear that Picard instigated the attack. When it is finally revealed that there was no profit to be gained in this encounter, Bok is disgraced and stripped of his title. He would not be seen again until the seventh season.

The writers present the Ferengi as impressive villains. It is better written than "The Last Outpost." The slightly above average story poorly portrays Ferengi, but offers more good background of Picard.

EPISODE TEN: "HIDE AND Q"

Teleplay by C.J. Holland and Gene Roddenberry
Story by C.J. Holland
Directed by Cliff Bole
Guest Cast: John deLancie, Elaine Nalee, William A. Wallace

plague ship, he wastes little time before beaming over, rendering the wedding plot pointless.

The wedding gives Troi something to do. Female characters were badly written in the first season, so Denise Crosby chose to leave the show. The episode should have focused on Wyatt and the plague ship without the wedding nonsense as the two plotlines never converge.

One pointless scene shows that Riker has feelings for Troi and is disturbed by her impending marriage. Yet when the wedding is canceled, Riker never looks Troi's way again for years! The sixth season episode "Second Chances" finally resolves this relationship.

They finally learned to use one, coherent storyline late in season one. "Haven" offers only a ridiculous story that opens with a talking piece of luggage and goes downhill.

Majel Barrett plays her recurring role as Troi's mother for laughs. Unfortunately, the writers again confused obnoxious with funny.

EPISODE TWELVE: "THE BIG GOODBYE"

Written by Tracy Torme
Directed by Joseph L. Scanlan
Guest Cast: Mike Genovese, Dick Miller, Carolyn Alport, Rhonda Aldrich, Eric Cord, Lawrence Tierney, Harvey Jason, William Boyett, David Selburg, Gary Armagnal

The holodeck appeared in the first episode, but its potential was first explored in this teleplay. It is a good episode, but not one of the best, although it won the Peabody Award for best dramatic teleplay. I attended a presentation by Gene Roddenberry when he announced the award, two days before the news appeared in the press. Roddenberry was fiercely proud and defensive of NEXT GENERATION since it had received well deserved drubbing during the first season. This award exonerated him in his own eyes, if not those of many critics.

The holodeck creates personalities who seem to have a life of their own. The idea spawned two memorable sequels, "Elementary, Dear Data" and "Moriarty." This inventive story was the first episode crafted entirely around an adventure in the holodeck. It introduced popular hard-boiled detective Dixon Hill, an obvious tip of the hat to mystery writer Raymond Chandler. Inexplicably TV GUIDE criticized it as being derivative of "A Piece of the Action" from the original STAR TREK just weeks before it garnered the Peabody Award for originality!

This salute to hard-boiled detective fiction goes deeper than the superficial idea first suggests. It proposes that the holograms created by the holodeck have personalities independent of their programming. The mechanism for this is never explained. Something is clearly wrong when an Enterprise crew man receives a real bullet wound and the other visitors to this "imaginary" setting are held captive.

Holograms refuse to accept their situation. Two put it to the ultimate test and are destroyed, although it is not clear what would happen if the deck recreated the characters. This episode demonstrated that the series had strong potential.

EPISODE THIRTEEN: "DATALORE"

Teleplay by Robert Lewin and Gene Roddenberry
Story by Robert Lewin and Maurice Hurley
Directed by Rob Bowman
Guest Cast: Biff Yeager

If any storyline strangled NEXT GENERATION in the cradle, it was this one. They return to the planet where Data was found, and discover the secret laboratory where the android was created. The episode then introduces an Evil Twin story.

Virtually every low grade TV series of the past twenty years has done an "evil twin" story. Stuck for an idea? Turn to an "evil twin" story! Satirists zero in on the evil twin syndrome. Jay Leno offered a great routine on the subject. The comic strip "Doonesbury" included an evil twin of George Bush. This episode treats it seriously.

The very phrase "evil twin" has become a joke, yet the original coming attractions for this episode refer to Lore as "Data's evil twin." Gene Roddenberry proudly put his name on this script. It has all the depth of LOST IN SPACE.

Data's creator is scientist "Noonian Soong." Roddenberry used the name because it is similar to that of a friend he knew in the service in the 1940s. Roddenberry hoped his lost friend would hear the name and contact him, but he never did.

Cooler heads prevailed. Lore appeared in three additional episodes in seven seasons, and two were the two-part storyline "Descent." It supposedly wrote finis to the cliché.

EPISODE FOURTEEN: "ANGEL ONE"

Teleplay by Patrick Berry
Directed by Michael Rhodes
Guest Cast: Karen Montgomery, Sam Hennings, Leonard John Crowfoot, Patricia McPherson,

Before this episode aired, I heard production had been shut down for a day while the script was reworked. It still suffers from 20th Century anachronisms, including "Bingo!" and "Will you still respect me in the morning?" Why the writer repeats clichés is puzzling. The challenge is to avoid clichés and create interesting dialogue.

Some stories are clichés in science fiction. One is the society ruled by women, whether Amazons or modern "feminist" science fiction. It has taken on unsavory political connotations.

A female writer who contributed to an anthology of stories about female barbarians found herself accosted at a science fiction convention by another contributor. She believed the female writer "betrayed the lesbian separatist movement" by marrying her boyfriend. The writer never knew the movement existed.

"Angel One" entered this modern morass of clashing political ideologies. The story tries to have it both ways, postulating a matriarchal society in which men are subservient, while portraying a faction that wants to treat men as equals.

The female rulers do not wear metal breast plates or speak barbarian jargon. The thin plot sends the Enterprise searching for survivors of a Federation vessel that disappeared seven years earlier. Several men landed on the planet and mated with women who preferred strong males. It led to an underclass of separatist women opposed to the matriarchal society. Those in charge find them abhorrent and threatening. The ruler demonstrates compassion by sparing the men and their wives from execution, exiling them to live in peace.

Instead of developing the ideas, Roddenberry apparently insisted the "Enterprise be in jeopardy" so a plague sweeps through the vessel. Dr. Crusher must find a cure before Riker and the away team can return to the ship.

EPISODE FIFTEEN: "11001001"

Written by Maurice Hurley and Robert Lewin
Directed by Paul Lynch
Guest Cast: Carolyn McCormack, Iva Lane, Kelli Ann McNally, Jack Sheldon, Abdul Salaam El Razzac, Ron Brown, Gene Dynarski, Katy Boyer, Alexandra Johnson

This episode is a turning point completely different from the original STAR TREK. It is also a very good story.

The Enterprise is in jeopardy. Two members of an alien race, the Binars, steal the ship. Riker and Picard don't know it because they're involved in the holodeck.

While previous episodes valiantly, but hopelessly, focused on all nine of the ensemble cast, they soon had to spotlight fewer players. Picard and Riker became firmly established as the primary leads in this episode. Data soon joined them. Worf fluctuated between main and supporting character, while Geordi, Troi, Yar, Doctor Crusher and Wesley brought up the rear. Denise Crosby saw the writing on the wall and soon left.

This tight, well-crafted story begins as Picard and Riker learn they are on a stolen Enterprise bound for an unknown destination. They decide to destroy the ship.

It turns out the vessel wasn't stolen for villainous reasons. The Binars are linked with the computer on their world. They need the computers of a starship to reboot their master computer. They stole the vessel and plan to face the consequences.

This is a refreshing change. It presents the "things aren't always what they seem" motif by revealing the benevolent intentions of the aliens. The aliens even return to Starfleet to answer for their crimes.

A female hologram named Minuet provides an imaginative touch. Riker finds the fantasy of more than passing interest. There is genuine chemistry between the two. We feel Riker's sense of loss when Minuet disappears along with the rest of the Binars' stored information.

The episode revealed that Riker, and Jonathan Frakes, enjoy playing the trombone.

EPISODE SIXTEEN: "TOO SHORT A SEASON"

Teleplay by Michael Michaelian and D.C. Fontana
Story by Michael Michaelian
Directed by Rob Bowman
Guest Cast: Clayton Rohner, Marsha Hunt, Michael Pataki

Scripts in early NEXT GENERATION episodes ran wildly inconsistent. It is exemplified here. Somewhere in this mishmash of youth drugs, vengeance and a tale of one last hurrah is the germ of a good idea. Bad acting by Clayton Rohner as Admiral Mark Jameson further ruins a bad script.

The episode starts as a story of an old man who overdoses on a youth drug for reasons other than the threat he faces. Then it begins a cloudy morality tale about an aging statesman who faces the war he caused by betrayal 45 years before when he secretly violated the Prime Directive.

The makeup for Jameson is terrible. The actor portrays the old man as a cartoon parody. He can't say a line without breathing tension as though every muscle is tied in knots while imitating a young Marlon Brando or James Dean.

Jameson and his old nemesis finally come face to face without fiery oratory because he drops dead on the spot. It was obvious ten minutes into the show that Jameson would die, killing the surprise.

The episode is about the guest star with the regulars along for the ride. This would not be a bad change of pace if the guest star were interesting, but everything remains underdeveloped. They needed a new, logical script.

Admiral Jameson could have taken the youth drug without overdosing and still confronted Karnas. He didn't have to look like 25 again for the confrontation. The adversaries could have debated the events of 45 years before. Jameson would have faced the consequences of his actions. Instead of ending a war, he prolonged it by secretly arming both sides.

Having Jameson drop dead at the end is just a clean way to wrap up a sloppy story.

EPISODE SEVENTEEN: "WHEN THE BOUGH BREAKS"

Teleplay by Hannah Louise Shearer
Directed by Kim Manners

Guest Cast: Dierk Torsek, Michele Marsh, Dan Mason, Philip N. Waller, Connie Danese, Jessica and Vanessa Bova, Jerry Hardin, Brenda Strong, Jandi Swanson, Paul Lambert, Ivy Bethune

Fans debated the wisdom of having children on the Enterprise. This episode settled the issue. The Enterprise encounters a legendary planet. The advanced native race faces extinction because they have become sterile. Picard refuses to sell them children so they steal some from the Enterprise.

The story makes no sense. They only kidnap seven children to repopulate an entire race. They could have surmounted this problem by using sperm and eggs removed from the healthy kidnap victims and grown in a crèche system. That is never addressed in the episode.

Aldeans see nothing morally wrong in trading goods or services for children. They're annoyed that Picard finds it repugnant. An interesting idea was executed clumsily. The episode fails to explore the cultural differences.

A good scene occurs near the end. One child benefited from the experience. She learned art from the Aldeans. It's a good touch and ends the episode on a thoughtful note.

EPISODE EIGHTEEN: "HOME SOIL"

Teleplay by Robert Sabaroff
Story by Karl Guers, Ralph Sanchez and Robert Sabaroff
Directed by Corey Allen
Guest Cast: Walter Gotell, Elizabeth Lidsey, Mario Roccuzzo, Carolyn Barry, Gerard Pendergast

Terraforming takes bleak, lifeless planets and transforms them into thriving worlds with florae and fauna from Earth. The painstaking process alters a planet's atmosphere and chemical balances. It might be possible to do this to Mars now, but it would take hundreds of years.

Scientists in this episode carefully scanned a planet for native life forms before beginning the process. They later discover a microscopic native life form after 20 years of work, but they want to hide the information rather than jeopardize their project.

The story, like "Justice," offers a lop-sided argument. The microscopic life form is intelligent and capable of communication. This leaves no room for debate. If the amoebas weren't intelligent it would have raised more interesting questions. The flawed story is better than average for first season NEXT GENERATION.

EPISODE NINETEEN: "COMING OF AGE"

Written by Sandy Fries
Directed by Michael Vejar

Guest stars: Estee Chandler, Daniel Riordan, Brendan McKane, Wyatt Knight, Ward Costello, Robert Schekkan, Robert Ito, John Putch, Stephan Gregory, Tasia Valenza

Parallel storylines relate to Starfleet in this episode. Wesley is tested for admission in an imaginative but unrealistic plotline. Only one candidate can be selected each year. Why should talented people be rejected to try again the next year? It would make more sense to accept all that score exceptionally well on a variety of tests rather than choosing only the most exceptional of a very talented group. The logic is never adequately explained and appears to be a conceit of the writer.

Wesley undergoes a "psyche" test and must face his deepest fear. It is a good scene. We're left wondering what the deepest fears of the other candidates are? Showing what they went through would have been enlightening. Wesley's test requires him to choose which of two lives to save. The compelling situation must often occur in Starfleet. This was how his father died. That made it his personal cross to bear.

While Wesley undergoes his baptism of fire, Captain Picard is grilled for decisions made earlier in the season. Dropped plotlines are confronted head on in a dramatic and satisfying manner. It demonstrates series continuity and sense of self. Most TV shows never refer to past episodes. Thankfully NEXT GENERATION didn't follow that design.

This episode possesses a strong emotional undertone elevating it above typical TV science fiction fare. The series was definitely showing signs of great improvement.

EPISODE TWENTY: "HEART OF GLORY"

Teleplay by Maurice Hurley
Story by Maurice Hurley and Herb Wright & D.C. Fontana
Directed by Rob Bowman
Guest Cast: Vaughn Armstrong, Robert Bauer, Brad Zerbst, Dennis Madalone, Charles H. Hyman

This episode introduced the Klingon Empire as allies of the Federation. NEXT GENERATION opened up many new possibilities, including further defining the Klingons. Klingons were all villains in the original STAR TREK. The strong code of honor of 24th Century Klingons didn't motivate most 23rd Century Klingons. Klingon 24th Century culture is revealed in detail in this episode.

Before "Heart of Glory" Worf added color but little depth to the series. This was the first of several Klingon episodes. They appeared once, sometimes twice, each season. It showed Worf in an interesting light, as a proud warrior who believes in the honor and tradition of his culture even though raised by humans. Other Klingons view him with suspicion because he was raised by humans. Worf won't tolerate questioning of his beliefs in his Klingon heritage.

The Enterprise rescues three Klingons from a disabled vessel. The warriors distrust humans and only feel comfortable around Worf. They question Worf's affiliation with Starfleet, but he articulately explains his reasons. A bond forms between the warriors. When one of the three dies of injuries sustained before being rescued, a new aspect of Klingon culture appears. It works perfectly.

The Klingon death chant chills with intense personal emotion. Expressions on the faces of Worf's human friends show surprise and inner questioning better than dialogue could. When Worf and the other two warriors shout a warning that a Klingon is on his way to the realm beyond life, we finally see that a Klingon doesn't just look different from a human being. They are profoundly different.

The other Klingons are outlaws who despise peace with the Federation because they want to die in combat. Death from old age, or in one's sleep, is the worst dishonor a Klingon can endure. These Klingon throwbacks still have dimension. When crewmen arrest them, they appear about to take a child hostage. Then they reveal that their sense of personal honor prevents them from warring on children. It's a very good scene, in an episode with many good scenes.

These are the first Klingons to appear in NEXT GENERATION other than Worf. They hold different views than most modern day Klingons. This creates drama through intensely personal conflict for Worf. He has had few opportunities to be with his own people. If Worf had encountered more diplomatic Klingons, the clash of wills would not have been evident. Conflict forces Worf to deal with the gulf between himself and these two members of his own race and the vast cultural differences with his fellow crewmen.

The episode reveals previously unseen potential in the character and leaves other regulars looking pale by comparison.

EPISODE TWENTY-ONE: "ARSENAL OF FREEDOM"

Teleplay by Richard Manning and Hans Beimler
Story by Maurice Hurley and Robert Lewin
Directed by Les Landau
Guest Cast: Vincent Schiavelli, Marco Rodriguez, Vyto Ruginis, Julia Nickson, George De La Pena

This episode failed to develop interesting ideas in more than a superficial manner. It appeared hurriedly written and rushed into production.

The simplistic core notion is reminiscent of the original STAR TREK. A planet of high tech weapons brokers is wiped out by automated weapons when they get out of control. This very "Sixties" notion seems to bear Gene Roddenberry's fingerprints. It plays like an early first season episode. One main credited writer worked on "Heart of Glory."

Picard joins the away team, along with Dr. Crusher. When the team is attacked, they're cut off from the Enterprise, placing the Enterprise in jeopardy, a Roddenberry favorite. Parallel stories of the Enterprise in peril and the away team in danger work, but there's no emotional frission.

An entire planet's population has been destroyed, but we don't care about them as people. When Riker encounters a friend, he discovers it's just an imitation. He doesn't show emotion after learning the man must be dead. It's all very cool and by the numbers; action adventure without the necessary human equation to give it real impact.

The first season, particularly in the Roddenberry rewrites, hinted at a relationship between Dr. Crusher and Captain Picard. The hints appear here, but the story quickly veers away from it.

At one point Dr. Crusher, the least developed main character in the seven years of the series, starts revealing the story of a tragedy in the colony where she grew up. Then another robot suddenly attacks, and she never finishes her story!

We learn nothing about the society or the previous Federation ship that were destroyed. Riker expresses no grief over the death of his friend, the ship's captain. A budding relationship between Picard and Dr. Crusher is abandoned midstream. It is a disappointing episode.

EPISODE TWENTY-TWO: "SYMBIOSIS"

Teleplay by Robert Lewin, Richard Manning, and Hans Beimler
Story by Robert Lewin
Directed by Win Phelps
Guest Cast: Merritt Butrick, Judson Scott, Kimberly Farr, Richard Lineback

The Prime Directive is fundamental to Federation law. It is also an easy way out when difficult ethical judgments must be made. This episode masquerades as a typical anti-drug polemic complete with Wesley naively asking why someone would want to ingest something that could harm them.

Getting high gets a new definition in this story. Drugs hook people in a particularly pernicious way. It directly correlates to runaway capitalism.

The Enterprise discovers a planet addicted to a drug. The people believe it is a serum against a plague that ravaged their world hundreds of years ago. While the plague is long dead, the population is now addicted. They think the plague is returning when someone doesn't take their regular dose and dies. They don't realize they are dying from addiction withdrawal.

A neighboring world supplies the drug. They know what they're doing but the commerce of their planet depends on selling vast quantities of the drug. They only have one customer.

The usual dialogue about drug addiction is pointless. These aren't recreational hallucinogens or mood changers. The addicts believe good feelings arise from defeating plague symptoms.

If they wanted to do a story about a social problem, drugs are the safest subject. Interesting ideas are explored but not resolved. Picard ultimately resorts to the Prime Directive and refuses to get involved. That forces the issue between the two cultures. Picard doesn't stick around to see if they solve the problem or just destroy each other.

EPISODE TWENTY-THREE: "SKIN OF EVIL"
Teleplay by Joseph Stefano and Hannah Louise Shearer
Story by Joseph Stefano
Directed by Joseph L. Scanlan
Guest Cast: Walker Boone, Brad Zerbst, Raymond Forchion, Mart McChesney and Ron
Gans as the voice of Armus

Denise Crosby became increasingly unhappy with the handling of her character. She left the series. She may have jumped the gun as the show underwent growing pains and character development, particularly of females, took a long time to appear.

Fans knew this story was in the works, but it failed to live up to expectations. Deanna Troi is trapped inside a crashed shuttle craft by the black blob that killed Tasha Yar in the first act. The episode then drags on until Troi's rescue. The thing is left to rot on the barren world.

The best part occurs in the final scenes in the holodeck where Tasha's funeral is held. A line cut from the show had the Tasha hologram speak to Data, saying, "Data, it did happen," a reference to their sexual liaison in "The Naked Now."

The main storyline of an ancient embodiment of evil marooned on a barren planet had many parallels to STAR TREK V—THE FINAL FRONTIER. Neither is well developed.

Tasha's death was so pointless everyone later decided she deserved a better send-off. She got it in "Yesterday's Enterprise" two years later. Denise Crosby had second thoughts and turned up in season four as Tasha's daughter, then made a final appearance in the series finale, "All Good Things" when scenes from "Encounter At Farpoint" were recreated.

Tasha Yar deserved better. She could have developed into a very compelling character if given the chance.

EPISODE TWENTY-FOUR: "WE'LL ALWAYS HAVE PARIS"
Teleplay by Deborah Dean Davis and Hannah Louise Shearer
Directed by Robert Becker
Guest stars: Isabel Lorca, Rod Loomis, Dan Kern, Jean-Paul Vignon, Kelly Ashmore, Lance Spellerberg, Michelle Phillips

Science fiction shows often toy with time travel. This was the first NEXT GENERATION episode to deal with it. The results are mixed.

The Enterprise investigates time distortions caused by a scientist's experiments. Picard is distracted by the scientist's wife, an old flame of his. The excellent plot would have been more compelling had it dealt in a linear fashion with the time distortions. Instead it takes side trips to see Picard wring his hands over the girl he left behind in a Paris restaurant, and who has now turned up here at the end of the galaxy. The imaginative story is so well handled that the subplot with Picard and Mrs. Mannheim ultimately doesn't intrude.

They took the title from CASABLANCA, a film in which two old lovers unexpectedly encounter each other in an out of the way place after parting in Paris. The episode uses it as a typical old flame subplot. Good character stories for Picard should appear, but this is flat.

The time paradoxes are fascinating, particularly the scenes when Data is sent in to do what only he can accomplish. This story spotlights Data in a dramatic and creative fashion. The highly entertaining action-adventure episode is better than average. Later first year episodes demonstrate better plotting. The subplot with Picard's old flame significantly effects the main plotline. This is far more satisfying than another power failure on the Enterprise.

EPISODE TWENTY-FIVE: "CONSPIRACY"

Teleplay by Tracy Torme
Story by Robert Sabaroff
Directed by Cliff Bole
Guest Cast: Michael Berryman, Ursaline Bryant, Henry Darrow, Robert Schenkkan, Jonathan Farwell

This compelling, controversial story is genuinely scary at times. It catches the faint of heart by surprise at its climax. THE NEXT GENERATION played it safe until this point. Nothing was even remotely disturbing until "Conspiracy."

Gene Roddenberry had been critical of science fiction that automatically made ugly aliens evil. Here a nasty race of creatures crawl inside human beings through their mouth and control their brains. They want to control Starfleet and the entire Federation.

The plot unfolds as Picard secretly meets an old friend. It builds suspense layer upon layer until the strange climax. State of the art makeup effects eviscerate a man controlled by the queen alien before our eyes. Nothing like that had ever appeared on TV outside of the cable movie channels. A couple of years earlier, they cut all the special makeup effects when THE THING (1982) appeared on network television. The "Conspiracy" offered special effects as disturbing as anything CBS censored.

Graphic violence in the climax startles the viewer. It upset some people. That's to be expected when you take risks. At heart this is an old-fashioned alien invasion story, but it delivers a tight plot, inner tension and a sense that the characters are involved in real danger. This mood of impending destruction has rarely been attempted since.

The alien conspiracy story ended with a mysterious coded message beamed into an unknown region of space, but the series never followed up on this. It was left unresolved. Writers of official STAR TREK novels were forbid this loose story thread. Seemingly someone wanted to tie-up this story, but never quite got around to it.

EPISODE TWENTY-SIX: "THE NEUTRAL ZONE"

SEASON ONE

Written by Maurice Hurley
From a story by Deborah McIntyre and Mona Clee
Directed by James L. Conway
Guest Cast: Marc Alaimo, Anthony James, Leon Rippy, Gracie Harrison

The Romulans re-emerge at the end of this episode, bearing promises of more to come. The plot reveals that 20th Century people could be frozen when they died, with plans to be thawed out and brought back to life when the technology became available. One 20th Century company put the "corpsicles" into a huge satellite and launched it into space. One of these old satellites is found by the Enterprise.

Three 20th Century humans are found in suspended animation. The primary plot deals with their revival and attempts to adjust to the 24th Century. One of the three, a wealthy 20th Century man, finds that none of his wealth remains in the 24th Century. It was spent by his descendants. He must start over. Talk about future shock!

The Enterprise encounters Romulans when both explore mysteriously destroyed outposts along the Neutral Zone. It wouldn't be resolved until the Borg enter the NEXT GENERATION universe some time later.

The Romulans appear as an afterthought. Their use demonstrated the vital element they are in the 24th Century. Original STAR TREK used Romulans sparingly and revealed little about them. THE NEXT GENERATION put them at the heart of interesting episodes as they turned into more than stock villains.

Marc Alaimo played one of the Romulans. He later turned up as the Cardassian, Gul Dukat, in DEEP SPACE NINE.

SEASON

TWO

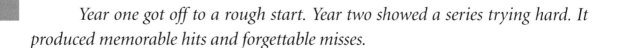

Year one got off to a rough start. Year two showed a series trying hard. It produced memorable hits and forgettable misses.

SEASON TWO

EPISODE TWENTY-SEVEN: "THE CHILD"

Written by Jaron Summer, Jon Povil and Maurice Hurley
Directed by Rob Bowman
Guest Cast: Seymour Cassel, R.J. Williams, Dawn Arnemann, Zachary Benjamin, Dore Keller
Introducing Diana Muldaur as Dr. Pulaski.
Introducing Whoppi Goldberg as Guinan.

A writer's strike delayed the start of the fall TV season. When it ended, NEXT GENERATION saved time by dusting off unused scripts from the never produced 1977 STAR TREK II series. They hurriedly changed them to a TNG script. The weak result provided an inauspicious beginning for the second season.

Doctor Pulaski joined the crew in this episode. Starfleet supposedly transferred Dr. Crusher to Medical. They never adequately explain why her son remained behind.

Whoopi Goldberg's Guinan proved to be a more interesting addition to the cast. Film pressures require the actress to keep her appearances irregular. She still enjoys more good scenes in the second season than Diana Muldaur's Dr. Pulaski. The writers found the doctor hard to write. She abruptly departed after the second season.

An alien impregnates Deanna so it can be born into human form and learn about this new race. Deanna gives birth in a 36 hours. The child becomes the equivalent of eight years old in 48 hours. Deanna bonds with the child. When circumstances force it to resume its normal non-corporeal form, Deanna is grief stricken.

They should have followed up on this in subsequent episodes. It isn't normal to recover from such emotional strain so quickly, even in the 24th Century. She should have displayed remorse by either wanting a real son or revealing a fear of having children because they might die, too. It's an uneven start to the second season.

EPISODE TWENTY-EIGHT: "WHERE SILENCE HAS LEASE"

Written by Jack B. Sowards
Directed by Winrich Kolbe
Guest Cast: Earl Boen, Charles Douglas

A strange alien entity traps the Enterprise in this creaky storyby. It uses the vessel and its crew as cosmic lab rats.

The coming attractions looked exciting. They showed Riker and Worf battling monstrous aliens. That proved to be a holodeck exercise depicted in the teaser. It's all downhill from there. The Enterprise encounters repetitious illusions and replicas after being lured into a featureless void.

The alien wants to experiment with death and plans to kill a third of the crew. Picard acts out of character. Rather than surrendering, he sets the auto destruct mechanism to destroy the Enterprise. This confounds the alien, forcing it to let the people go.

This entire story takes place on the ship with no stopovers at new worlds. It fails to effectively depict the principal characters. With the Enterprise facing imminent destruction, there should have been more internal conflicts, particularly with families on the vessel. Picard never shows how he feels about giving a death sentence to children. Many ideas were left untouched in this dreary episode.

The alien contacts Picard and tries to be friendly in a good scene at the end. Picard angrily rejects it. It has needlessly killed one of his crew. The amiable Picard obviously possesses a quick temper when faced with unreasonable opposition. At least he's learned that surrendering isn't always the best choice.

EPISODE TWENTY-NINE: "ELEMENTARY, DEAR DATA"

Written by Brian Alan Lane
Directed by Rob Bowman
Guest Cast: Daniel Davis, Alan Shearman, Biff Manard, Diz White, Anne Ramsay, Richard Merson

The holodeck has been used in imaginative ways. "The Big Goodbye" paid tribute to writers Raymond Chandler and Dashiel Hammett with the invention of the hard-boiled detective Dixon Hill. This episode tops that by recreating Sherlock Holmes, portrayed by none other than that master of deduction, Data. Geordi tags along as Watson.

Since Data has memorized all the Sherlock Holmes stories, their holodeck recreations go through the motions without solving mysteries. "The Big Goodbye" revealed that the holodeck could have unpredictable side effects. This episode takes that one step further.

When Data realizes he can't solve a mystery if he knows the outcome, Geordi programs Prof. Moriarty with enough knowledge to outsmart Data. The wrinkle? Moriarty becomes self-aware because Geordi should have told the computer to give Moriarty enough knowledge to outsmart Sherlock Holmes rather than Data.

Prof. Moriarty's legend grew as large as that of Holmes over the years, even though he only appeared in one of Doyle's original stories, "The Final Problem." He was the only traditional villain Holmes ever faced. All the others were spies and other ordinary criminals. Moriarty ran the greatest crime ring in England. Doyle never returned to the character but films and pastiche writers frequently resurrected the delightful villain.

Actor Daniel Davis brought Moriarty to life for NEXT GENERATION. This time the 19th Century mastermind possesses 24th Century knowledge. He challenges Data by kidnapping Dr. Pulaski, but he has grander plans. With the knowledge Data inadvertent-ly told the computer to give him, Moriarty takes control of the Enterprise through the holodeck. Moriarty knows he's a hologram and wants real life.

The computer did not create an evil Moriarty. This Moriarty, unlike the original, can be appealed to on humane terms. Picard promises to give the hologram true physical life when they know how. Moriarty agrees to wait.

The sequel to this story waited until season six because the copyrights on Sherlock Holmes are not entirely in public domain in the United States, although they are in England, the country of origin. Since "The Final Problem" is in public domain, it was deemed safe to reuse the Prof. Moriarty character.

EPISODE THIRTY: "THE OUTRAGEOUS OKONA"

Teleplay by Burton Armus
Story by Les Menchen, Lance Dickson and Kieran Mulroney
Directed by Robert Becker
Guest Cast: William O. Campbell, Douglas Rowe, Albert Stratton, Joe Piscopo

This is as bad as the worst of the first season. They had named the blob-like crea-ture in "Skin of Evil" after this writer, Burton Armus, supposedly as a tribute.

The Enterprise picks up a stranded wayfarer, and finds itself in a dispute over a stolen jewel and a complaint from another party. The other party insists that Okona impregnated a young lady. Okona is innocent of both charges. The story focuses on the guest star instead of the main characters. Unfortunately the guest star isn't very interest-ing.

Because Okona tells jokes, Data wants to learn humor. One wonders if Data ever heard any of his friends tell jokes. Are his friends so stiff that he has first encountered humor now? Unfortunately, to learn humor, Data has the holodeck create a hologram of Joe Piscopo to tell jokes. Is the future really going to deem Joe Piscopo a master of come-dy?

He's supposed to teach Data how to tell jokes. They needed someone to teach Joe Piscopo how to tell jokes, or to get better material. Supposedly the producers wanted Jerry Lewis, but he wasn't available.

A dreary episode. Give it a pass.

EPISODE THIRTY-ONE: "LOUD AS A WHISPER"

Written by Jacqueline Zambrano
Directed by Larry Shaw
Guest Cast: Howie Seago, Marnie Mosiman, Thomas Oglesby, Leo Damian

This episode offered the most unusual idea ever conceived for STAR TREK. It introduces the deaf mute Riva, a famed negotiator. He brings his "chorus," three people who express his thoughts and feelings and maintain constant mental contact with him. The four individuals are linked as one.

This appeared three years before STAR TREK VI: THE UNDISCOVERED COUNTRY, creating a continuity problem. Riva was supposedly the architect of the Klingon-Federation peace treaty. That treaty was hammered out in the 23rd Century, making Riva look remarkably good for his age. Perhaps his is a long-lived race?

The character wasn't referred to in THE UNDISCOVERED COUNTRY, but by 1991 they were having trouble keeping continuity straight.

Howie Seago, a deaf-mute actor, played Riva. His performance was quite good, particularly when tragedy strikes late in the story and he is cut off from the world he carefully nurtured. This could have been explored in more detail. The ending leaves much unresolved.

The thin teleplay doesn't support the imaginative concept. On one level the episode is a remarkable effort, but on another it's a misfire.

[ADDITIONAL COMMENTARY BY WENDY RATHBONE]

The "chorus" concept is illuminated in a fascinating way by the actors. The three chorus members represent the scholar-dreamer-poet, the passion-libido-warrior, and, the only female, harmony-wisdom-balance, the third that binds them all together. Riva has had his Chorus for a long time. They are so finely attuned to him that there appears to be no delay between thought and speaking. The writing is superb. Riva is one of the most fascinating characters to board the Enterprise.

I did not like that Worf feels hostility toward Riva because Riva mediated Klingon-Federation disputes. Worf says before Riva there was no Klingon word for "peacemaker." This history happened before Worf was born. Worf's hostility appears to be bigotry. It makes no sense coming from a Starfleet officer raised by humans.

Worf is irritating in the early episodes. He inherited old-fashioned Klingon ways while living in a modern world. Although our current world shows this is possible, it's irritating.

The scene when Worf acts hostile is a complete throwaway. It has nothing to do with the episode or the plot.

Riva is quite taken with Troi. He forcefully pursues her and fawns over her, but she likes it. They have dinner together, with the "passion" of the chorus interpreting. Later, "passion" leaves and Riva and Troi use hand signals to communicate.

Riva, Riker and Worf beam down to the planet to set up a meeting site. The warring factions arrive. A man opposed to peace fires a gun at Riva. Riker tackles Riva. The blast misses them but disintegrates the chorus. We get to see their skeletons before they vanish. The chorus is an endearing aspect of Riva. It is quite shocking to watch them die.

Pulaski thinks she can give Geordi normal vision in a totally unrelated plot flaw. There is no follow up. The scene should have been cut from the episode. It has nothing to do with anything, except that it parallels Riva's handicap and prosthesis. It takes away from the grief and emotion of the Riva story.

Troi convinces Riva that he can still negotiate without his chorus. This very powerful, intellectual scene keeps emotions at bay. Riva never sheds a tear over the chorus. He only says they were his friends and he misses them deeply. That is communicated only through dialogue.

The actor who plays Riva, Howie Sego, is actually deaf, and he suggested the idea for this episode. The actress who plays the female chorus member denoting wisdom/harmony/balance is Marnie Mosiman, real-life wife of John DeLancie ("Q".)

I like this episode, despite its flaws. These include TNG's greatest flaw, a recurring failure to show emotions other than humor. The Worf and Geordi scenes should have been dropped. Otherwise, this is a great episode, based on a great idea. I'd like to see it taken a few steps further in future meetings with humanoids who use choruses to communicate.

EPISODE THIRTY-TWO: "UNNATURAL SELECTION"
Written by John Mason and Mike Gray
Directed by Paul Lynch
Guest Cast: Patricia Smith, J. Patrick McNamara, Scott Trost

After skipping retreads of the original STAR TREK for a time, this episode reworked the "Deadly Years." It lifted an ending from the "Deadly Years" take-off in the animated STAR TREK series.

It's a story about someone quickly aging. They need to reverse it. Original STAR TREK inflicted all the principal characters with the malady; this time it's just the doctor.

The opening is similar. In the original story, the Enterprise found a colony where everyone was either dead or dying of old age. This time the Enterprise responds to a distress call and finds a starship crew all dead of old age. This time it's not a virus. Genetically engineered children emit anti-bodies against external viruses. The anti-bodies inflict the aging disease.

Once Dr. Pulaski is quarantined, they determine that transporter records could reconstitute her. Unfortunately she has had an aversion to the transporter so no such records are available. How she always boarded the Enterprise without the transporter isn't explained.

This aversion to the transporter sounds familiar. Dr. McCoy had a similar aversion. Parts of Pulaski's personality seem grafted onto her from Dr. McCoy. She's gruff but likable, and just as ascerbic towards Data as McCoy was to Spock, although this aspect of her personality disappeared.

For some reason NEXT GENERATION replaced Gates McFadden with Diana Muldaur. It wasn't the best decision. This was the only episode to feature Dr. Pulaski. She disappeared into the background for the rest of season two.

[ADDITIONAL COMMENTARY BY WENDY RATHBONE]

Pulaski went to the Darwin station to die. The exterior of Darwin station looks gothic, a half-ruined building on the edge of a cliff during sunset. It's shown twice. I'd like to have the matte painting on my wall.

The disease is explained three times: Once, when Data and Pulaski discuss the theory; a second time, when they find their theory correct after computer research; and a third time, when a communication from the Darwin station informs Picard. It's sloppy writing.

The Enterprise crew, including Geordi, Picard, Riker, and O'Brien, use the transporter to filter the genetic change. It's all done with lots of pseudo-science and tongue-twisting words.

The cured Darwin station scientists can never return to their genetically created children. They don't seem to worry about leaving them behind. This makes little sense. They worry early in the episode because the children would die when left alone.

The weak story offers strong tension between Pulaski and Picard, who admire each other's talents. This episode is a little too similar to "The Deadly Years."

EPISODE THIRTY-THREE: "A MATTER OF HONOR"

Teleplay by Burton Armus
From a story by Wanda M. Haight, Gregory Amos and Burton Armus
Directed by Rob Bowman
Guest Cast: John Putch, Christopher Collins, Brian Thompson,

The second Klingon episode on NEXT GENERATION didn't center on Worf. It is the only Klingon episode from the human point of view.

A Federation exchange program allows Will Riker to temporarily transfer to a Klingon ship as first officer, second in command, just as he is on the Enterprise. Riker prepares for the assignment by sampling Klingon cuisine, including that squirming, worm-like dish called *gagh*. Riker spooning it down provides quite a sight to see.

Riker's new fellow crewmen on the Klingon vessel, the Pagh, test the puny human. Riker puts them in their place and never backs down, even when approached by two female warriors who enjoy baiting this human in their midst.

Riker seems different from before. The normally amiable man acts as abrasive as his comrades because he knows showing weakness would lose the respect of these warriors. Riker shows a temper. The episode contrasts mannered life aboard the Enterprise with the coarseness of Klingon warriors. Conflict creates drama making "A Matter Of Honor" the best second season episode. Things happen and threats are believable.

This episode builds to a satisfying climax. Riker follows the orders of his superior officer when the Klingon commander threatens to attack the Enterprise. The clever, well executed ending demonstrates how good the NEXT GENERATION can be.

The thirty-third episode shows main characters getting angry with comrades for the first time. It would be interesting to see Riker punch a fellow officer on the Enterprise as he did on the Klingon ship. That would catch everyone by surprise.

[ADDITIONAL COMMENTARY BY WENDY RATHBONE]

Riker volunteers to serve aboard a Klingon ship while he and Picard shoot targets on the holodeck. It looks fun.

A Benzite comes aboard to participate in the exchange program. He looks exactly like the Benzite in "Coming of Age." Wes thinks it's the same guy until the Benzite tells him he is a different person from the same genetic pool.

Putting a Benzite on the bridge offered possibilities. He looks and acts alien. He even fails to inform Picard of a dangerous anomaly. He feels he shouldn't tell anyone until he solves the problem. This seems illogical, but Benzites are very efficient, although not good team players. This Benzite learns to be a good teammate, something he can take back to his own culture. This subplot illustrates a clash of cultures.

Klingons love to eat blood pie and live worms. Riker forces himself to eat these delicacies before boarding the Klingon ship. Riker also learns that Klingon first officers assassinate their captains if they show signs of weakness. This allows all Klingon warriors to die with honor. Few grow old or feeble, a state loathed by Klingon warriors.

Riker gets into a fight aboard the Klingon ship. The second officer questions Riker's loyalty, so Riker beats him up. Riker wins respect. He soon learns that Klingons have a sense of humor, though, and the Klingons learn to appreciate his human strengths.

Riker finally returns command of the Klingon ship to the rightful captain. He can't just give command back. That would be dishonorable. He must let the captain hit him so he appears overpowered. This great scene offers humor and honor, especially since all the Klingons know he allows himself to be hit. Jonathan Frakes is a good actor with too little to do most of the time.

Klingons are a weird breed. Their code of honor seemed ridiculous, until I realized it is really no different than any culture that respects ritual. Still, the Klingons are often portrayed as stupid. Supposedly warriors are the most rigid in loathing weakness.

The Klingons show a humorous side, and perhaps, away from battle, even a gentle side, though they would never admit it. I like the humor in this episode, the Benzite's breathing device, and the way honor is upheld by Riker. I am troubled that the Klingon captain jumps to irrational conclusions. This is a plot weakness not fully thought through by the writers.

EPISODE THIRTY-FOUR: "THE MEASURE OF A MAN"

Written by Melinda M. Snodgrass
Directed by Robert Scheerer
Guest Cast: Amanda McBroom, Clyde Kusatsu, Brian Brophy

A trial determines if Data has human rights. THE NEXT GENERATION entered a new arena unexplored by the original STAR TREK. Data is the only android in Starfleet. Some bureaucrats decide to find out what makes him tick since no one else has successfully created such a complex android. Dr. Soong is presumed dead, so Starfleet believes they have to disassemble him.

Data demands his right to a Starfleet hearing. Picard argues against taking Data apart because of the android's delicate positronic brain. Memory and personality could disappear in the process, destroying what makes Data a unique individual.

Original STAR TREK settled fights with force. NEXT GENERATION uses words instead. This fine script by Melinda Snodgrass demonstrates how compelling a war of words can be. Each side eloquently explains its position, but Data makes his point best.

Starfleet isn't portrayed as a dark hat. They want many androids like Data performing jobs too hazardous for humans. The positive results could be incalculable, but do androids have rights? This one's rights were recognized the day he entered Starfleet.

This stirring episode shows that the Enterprise needn't be in jeopardy for effective drama. The story is pure NEXT GENERATION at its best.

[ADDITIONAL COMMENTARY BY WENDY RATHBONE]

I love the senior officers' poker games. This time Riker bluffs Data and wins a pot with a bad hand.

Picard meets an old friend, Phillipa Louvois, at Starbase 173. Tension between them plays well on the screen. They are attracted to each other, yet their history together seems stormy. Phillipa prosecuted Picard in the Stargazer court-martial. He accuses her o enjoying that job. She calls him a "pompous ass."

Commander Bruce Maddox's research into cybernetics led him to Data. He possesses an overpowering desire to disassemble the android to learn how to replicate him. Picard is horrified, but Maddox already has Data's transfer order. Data has no say, even though the experiment could destroy his personality.

Picard seeks Phillipa for legal help. She serves as Judge Advocate General of the starbase. If anyone can help Picard and Data, she can. Then she admits her hands are tied. She says Data can save himself only by quitting Starfleet.

I love the idea, and the logic. Rules and regulations followed to the letter make events believable. I perched on the edge of my seat to see how things would work out, how people would out-think each other, how rules could be bent to show the truth.

I also love the idea that Data collects "things" as personal possessions. His possessions include a hologram of Tasha Yar, indicating his feelings for her. Maddox pays a visit while Data packs his "things." Maddox is angry that Data is resigning.

Maddox wants to preserve and spread knowledge of how Data works. He believes he can give every starship a valuable officer. Maddox consults Phillipa, "Would you permit the Enterprise computer to refuse a refit?" She cannot dispute his logic and concludes that Starfleet owns Data.

Can Data, a sentient being, actually be property? Picard requests a hearing. Following Federation protocol on starbases without legal officers, Phillipa appoints

Picard Data's legal defender. She insists, according to the letter of the law, that Riker must prosecute, since he's the next senior ranking officer. If Riker refuses, she will not permit a hearing, and conclude that "Data is a toaster." What a great line, and what an insult to the intellect of Data. So Riker, in a great dramatic plot twist, fights against his own beliefs.

The trial begins. It resembles the classic Trek episode "Court-Martial" in many ways. Riker zealously prosecutes Data, knowing that if he fails to do his best, Phillipa will stop the proceeding and Data will automatically lose. Riker shuts Data off. Picard asks for a recess and seeks Guinan for advice. In her subtle, wise way, Guinan points out the true theme of the episode, Slavery. If Maddox creates an army of "Datas," he is creating a race of "disposable creatures," a race of slaves. Starfleet seeks new life, not the creation of slavery.

Data admits he has the hologram of Yar because she was special. He says she is special to him because of shared intimacy, a reference to "The Naked Now." Perhaps their physical relationship continued after that episode. It's an intriguing thought.

Picard says that the definition of "sentience" is vague. He insists there is no real difference between humans and Data that can be defined. Picard raises the issue of slavery. Phillipa rules that Data be given freedom to choose his path in life. The question of Data's soul is never answered. She can't even prove she has one, so Data wins.

This riveting episode offers first rate dialogue and powerful tension. It addresses important issues in an intelligent and passionate way. This is one of my favorite TNG episodes.

Data is very human. The machine as metaphor offers a clarification of humanity. We see the truth of ourselves, and how little we know about the spark of life.

EPISODE THIRTY-FIVE: "THE SCHIZOID MAN"

Teleplay by Tracy Torme
Story by Richard Manning and Hans Beimler
Directed by Les Landau
Guest Cast: W. Morgan Sheppard, Suzie Plakson, Barbara Alyn Woods

This is another Data episode. A man again demonstrates an unhealthy interest in Dr. Soong's favorite creation. A brilliant colleague claims that he taught Dr. Soong everything he knew.

The Enterprise responds to a distress call. They find a dying scientist living on a world cut off from everything, accompanied only by a young female assistant. She regards him as a father figure, but doesn't know the elderly scientist feels other desires.

Dr. Graves transfers his conscious into Data. Data expresses emotions, including jealousy when he sees Picard with Kareen. This story is about Dr. Graves stealing Data's body and a man warped when he finds that he's young and strong again, and possibly immortal.

He frightens his former assistant, Kareen, when he admits what he's accomplished, and by his confession of love.

Dr. Graves is a decent man. He finally realizes he is wrong and chooses to end it. The scientist, initially portrayed as an arrogant buffoon, shows true humanity saving Data when Picard and the others fail.

Although not as emotional a story as "Measure of a Man," it shows another side of Data.

[ADDITIONAL COMMENTARY BY WENDY RATHBONE]

They never tell how many days the crew members remain on Graves' World. Graves spends all his time alone with Data because he says he doesn't want to be around people. He discusses his philosophy of life and death, and wants to know if Data feels emotions.

Graves plans to transfer his dying essence into a computer to cheat death, but would rather transfer into Data. He does just that off camera. The episode never shows how the dying scientist overpowers Data. This is a problem.

Data acts strange. Graves loves his young, pretty assistant. He will give himself away because he cannot control himself. It's obvious before it happens.

I felt no passion from the characters, only an underlying sense of humor that seemed slightly out of place. It seems that when androids try to be human, they are very tragic or very funny. Or both.

The crew is suspicious. Deanna gives Data a psyche test. They project intriguing images from the subject's mind on a screen. The test shows that an alien personality inhabits Data.

Deanna seems to have trouble pronouncing words in this episode. She always speaks very slowly and distinctly. This is characteristic of the actress, but it seems to be more of a problem for her than usual.

Data is confined to quarters. He disobeys the order and goes to Ten Forward to see Kareen. Data throws himself at her, declaring his love in a passionless, anti-climactic and very aggressive way. He even breaks her wrist, not knowing his own strength.

The crew learns that Graves was working to bridge the gap between man and machine. They should have known this before arriving on Graves' World.

They discover that Graves put his genius into the Enterprise computer, but his consciousness is lost. Data remembers nothing. The writers seem to say that he had been like a "real" split personality, where one facet is unaware of the other.

Suzie Plakson plays the Vulcan doctor. She later played Alexander's mother and Worf's lover-wife. She now has a recurring role on the sitcom LOVE AND WAR.

EPISODE THIRTY-SIX: "THE DAUPHIN"
Written by Scott Rubinstein and Leonard Mlodinow
Directed by Rob Bowman

Guest Cast: Paddi Edwards, Jamie Hubbard, Madchen Amick, Cindy Sorenson, Jennifer Barlow

This Wesley episode tells a young love story and reminds the viewer that things aren't always what they seem. The Enterprise picks up Salia, a young woman who has lived in exile from her homeworld for 16 years. Wesley falls in love with her. The young woman is a princess. Her mentor and bodyguard, Anya, opposes Salia's interest in Wesley because Salia is the Dauphin returning to her home planet to take her rightful place as its ruler.

When Anya physically intervenes by transforming into a frightening creature, Picard locks her up. As too often happened in the first two seasons, Worf, the head of security, gets knocked around. Michael Dorn ultimately complained about this. The powerful Klingon warrior shouldn't be beaten up by guest stars on a regular basis.

Salia must ultimately turn her back on Wesley because of her duty to her home-world. Wesley belatedly learns that Salia only adopts the form of an adolescent girl to travel among humans. When Wesley sees her true form, he has to decide whether he loved Salia for herself or for what she appeared to be.

[ADDITIONAL COMMENTARY BY WENDY RATHBONE]

The Enterprise plays taxi in this story, picking up a girl destined to rule a world. She looks about 16, though the actress playing the part was ten years older. Salia and Wes feel instant mutual attraction. Her over-protective governess hints that there's a secret she's hiding.

Salia's arrival on Daled IV should bring peace. One faction in the conflict comes from the side of the planet always in night while the other lives in perpetual daylight. Salia's parents came from both sides.

The shape-shifting governess transforms into a teenage girl and a waist-high teddy bear. This removes the surprise from her later shift into a monster in sickbay.

Some cute scenes show Wes going to others for love life advice. Worf tells him, in a humorous bit, that Klingon women roar to get a man's attention, and throw heavy objects while the man reads love poetry and ducks a lot. Wes says he doesn't think that will work with Salia, so Worf tells him to go to her door and beg like a human. That's funny stuff.

Another humor scene involves Riker and Guinan demonstrating to Wes how to sweet talk your way into someone's good graces. When Riker tells Guinan he dreams of a galaxy where her eyes are the stars, she is clearly impressed. Wes leaves, clearly frustrated.

Then the governess changes into a monster because she believes that a patient being treated in sickbay has contagious encephalitis. She demands that the patient be killed to avoid contamination. Pulaski is understandably appalled.

The monster looks hokey, with big teeth and red eyes. It stands about eight feet tall. This scene is a ridiculous plot flaw. The governess carefully hid that she and, apparently, Salia, are shape-shifters. Her paranoia reveals her alien nature too easily. The roiling green troposphere of the planet where Salia lived, and the planet where she is going to rule, should have clued the Enterprise crew in that these couldn't be humans.

I like the scene on the holodeck when Wes shows Salia the different worlds he has visited. She sees all that she's missed in her isolated life. Awesome special effects included 110 shots layered onto each other. This work kept many people up nights.

Wes gets his first kiss.

Supposedly the trip took only a few hours, with a few more hours added for repairs. How could Wes have loved and lost so quickly and been so deeply affected?

I don't like the way the governess abandons Salia at the end, saying her job is finished when Salia reaches her homeworld.

Humor and special effects enhance this episode. Major plot holes and forced drama cause it to fail as a story.

EPISODE THIRTY-SEVEN: "CONTAGION"
Written by Steve Gerber and Beth Woods
Directed by Joseph L. Scanlan
Guest Cast: Thalmus Rasulala, Carolyn Seymour, Dana Sparks

The Romulans returned in the "The Neutral Zone." They appear again when the Enterprise enters the Neutral Zone in response to a distress call. The Enterprise discovers the ancient civilization of Iconia.

The story isn't about hiding and fighting. Instead it establishes a tradition for the series. The Federation and the Romulans conduct an ambivalent relationship, sometimes friends but other times enemies. This episode offered a bit of both.

Discovering an ancient civilization with technology more advanced than that of the 24th Century offers interesting possibilities. The question arises whether the technology would be accessible. ANALOG MAGAZINE once ran an interesting story about a ramjet that moved back in history only by a couple of decades. No one could get the thing moving fast enough to start the jets, or understand how you kept fuel in when it is open at both ends.

The technology of Iconia includes a transporter with a gateway that can be focused anywhere, without anyone on the other end being aware of it.

The episode effectively depicts the uneasy truce between the Romulans and the Federation. It begins to establish the Romulans as an on-going adversary. They are given considerable dimension.

[ADDITIONAL COMMENTARY BY WENDY RATHBONE]
The Enterprise encounters another starship, the Yamato. It is suffering a major systems failure. As Picard and Riker talk to the ship's captain, the Yamato suddenly overloads and blows up.

The episode presents an effective scene between Picard and Wes. Wes asks how the captain handles death. The deaths, particularly of the civilians on the Yamato, deeply trouble Wes. Good for him. He hasn't bought into the stoic routine yet.

This episode delivers one of my favorite quotes from all Trek, when Riker says: "Fate protects fools, little children and ships called Enterprise."

The Enterprise suffers from a computer virus they believe they contracted from the Yamato. They meet a Romulan ship suffering the same fate.

Riker considers evacuation, a good plot idea, but a little late. He thinks the Romulans prevent this option. This doesn't make sense. The ship has enough time to go to the planet where the Yamato was to search for a cure, but not enough time to go to a safe planet and evacuate? They risk the lives of over 1000 people.

Worf goes through the gateway to the scene of the Enterprise, and appears with the limp Data in tow on the bridge. They are surprised to see him, but don't question how he got there. Since the bridge has been out of communication with the away team, you'd think they'd want to know how Worf appeared out of thin air without beaming in.

This episode offers good suspense, including the appearance of the Romulans, an injured Data and Data's apparent death. The gateway special effects and alien technology work well, but something is lacking. Perhaps it's characterization.

The episode presented interesting ideas and good suspense but left me unmoved.

EPISODE THIRTY-EIGHT: "THE ROYALE"

Written by Keith Mills (Tracy Torme)
Directed by Cliff Bole
Guest Cast: Sam Anderson, Jill Jacobson, Leo Garcia, Noble Willingham

This strange misfire showed Hollywood's peculiar, inexplicable fascination with Las Vegas, as though putting a casino in a story automatically heightens interest. It doesn't.

The dreary story drags on and on as the Enterprise discovers 21st Century NASA debris orbiting a bleak world too far from Earth to have been reached by primitive space technology. Planetside they discover the Hotel Royale, a structure built by departed aliens for a NASA astronaut marooned there 300 years ago. It's all based on a paperback novel the astronaut carried.

The astronaut lived on that world for 38 years before dying of old age. The Royale continued to operate. The away team must become part of the recurring program before the doors will open and they can escape. This episode shook one's faith in the NEXT GENERATION.

Writer Tracy Torme devised "The Royale" before the cast had been signed for the series. By the time it reached the screen, a disgruntled Torme, already on his way out the door at Paramount, had replaced his name with the pseudonym "Keith Mills." Although there are amusing character moments in this episode, too many scenes fell flat.

Torme intended it as a comedy, but they lost his original idea. The stranded astronaut for whom the imaginary world was created was, in Torme's original concept, still alive when the away team arrived. He was the central character! Torme must have hated having his protagonist replaced with an ancient corpse.

This drastic switch caused the loss of Torme's original conclusion, in which the still-living astronaut decides to stay in his illusive world. They altered the story in fear that the guest star would steal the show. The notion that the characters were trapped in a hack-written pulp novel was not Torme's idea, either. He may have found its inclusion a fitting irony considering the rewriting that was done to his teleplay.

[ADDITIONAL COMMENTARY BY WENDY RATHBONE]

The away team finds themselves in an old-style casino. The Enterprise loses all communication with them when they enter. Thus far the story parallels the O.K. Corral illusion the Melkotians used on Kirk and Spock in "The Spectre of the Gun."

The away team learns that the hotel has been expecting them. Then a story unfolds in front of them, complete with badly written dialogue. Data notes that none of the people in the Royale emit life signs.

Data plays blackjack in a cute, humorous scene. It turns to horror when the team discovers they cannot leave, much as in the song "Hotel California." The story still parallels "Spectre of the Gun" as Kirk, Spock, McCoy and Scotty discovered they couldn't leave Tombstone.

Most of the people in the hotel won't talk to them, though Data does get two to talk at the blackjack table. Worf tries to phaser his way out, but it doesn't work. They're trapped.

Deanna tells Picard that Riker is feeling trapped. The scenes with Deanna are completely unnecessary. Her presence on the bridge often causes plots to lose momentum and suspense. This episode feels forced, as if written in one night. The characters are all emotionless.

Late in the episode, one character from the novel enters the Royale and kills another. Riker is mystified when the murderer, Mickey D., exits the hotel through the revolving doors. Why? It's already been established that the people are not living humans, and that the place is created to repeat the story.

The novel ends when foreign investors buy the hotel, leaving it in the charge of the manager. It's convenient that Data is a good gambler. The foreign investors are the away team. They gamble until they have enough money, then buy the hotel and leave.

EPISODE THIRTY-NINE: "TIME SQUARED"

Teleplay by Maurice Hurley
From a story by Kurt Michael Bensmiller
Directed by Joseph L. Scanlan

This time travel tale reverses the usual rules. It postulates that the future can be changed. A duplicate Picard from six hours in the future returns to prevent the destruction of the Enterprise.

A forewarned Picard keeps from repeating the mistake that killed the ship. Whether such actions create a parallel timeline is not addressed. The seventh season episode "Parallels" showed that there are many parallel realities.

Picard is emerging as the main character in the series. Gene Roddenberry had been determined to create an ensemble as he wanted to avoid the Captain Kirk syndrome in which William Shatner gained a creative stranglehold on STAR TREK. While Patrick Stewart certainly doesn't have a stranglehold on THE NEXT GENERATION, he certainly emerged as the main character, with both Data and Will Riker tying for second place. The movie STAR TREK: GENERATIONS centers on Captain Picard.

EPISODE FORTY: "THE ICARUS FACTOR"
Teleplay by David Assael and Robert L. McCullough
Story by David Assael
Directed by Robert Iscove
Guest Cast: Mitchell Ryan, Lance Spellerberg

Seven years of this series told little about the many relatives of the main characters. Picard's parents are deceased so we met his brother's family. Geordi's family appeared in season seven and we know Deanna's mother. This episode introduced Will Riker's estranged father.

Problems between parents and grown children often appear on TV shows, just as in real life. Riker and his father reconcile by episode's end, but they aren't ready to share Thanksgiving dinner.

This marks the first time Will Riker is offered his own command, and turns it down. It happens several times in subsequent episodes. Actor Jonathan Frakes wasn't comfortable with the reasons given. He once replied to a convention questioner, saying it was "Bad writing." That caused a storm in the home office. He was more careful about what he said in public after that.

The "B" story of this episode is more interesting than the main story. Worf is upset that this is the tenth anniversary of his second Age of Ascension, a Klingon ceremony in which he ran a gauntlet of Klingons with pain sticks. His friends offer to witness his celebration of the event in the holodeck.

Worf re-enacts the painful ritual. The scene helps establish Worf's Klingon heritage, again demonstrating how different his culture is from everyone else's on the Enterprise.

Both stories deal with a person facing their problems head on.

[ADDITIONAL COMMENTARY BY WENDY RATHBONE]

Riker is offered the USS Aries, and his father, Kyle, comes aboard the Enterprise. They don't like each other. Pulaski previously had an affair with the dad. She's been married three times.

Worf behaves abnormally. He offers to go with Riker if he takes the promotion. Riker opens up to Worf, telling him he doesn't sense good feelings from his father. Riker and Worf have a friendship, and this kind of scene is too rare on this series.

Tension grows between Riker and Kyle. Riker blames his father for his mother's death.

Troi meets Kyle in a good scene. She learns he has false humility, and that he is competitive with his son, perhaps even jealous. It makes it easier to sympathize with Riker. Riker has been on his own since the age of 15.

So far, I like this story. Both the father and son story and the Worf story deal with human issues and human feelings. It is a rare delight to watch human conflicts overcome rather than the usual technical disasters that threaten the ship.

Wes determines Worf's problem: it's the tenth anniversary of his first age of ascension. He gives Worf the Klingon celebration he deserves.

Later, in the episode "First Born," this event was called the second Age of Ascension.

The ceremony involves pain sticks. Klingons consider enduring pain to be a great strength.

In a surprise plot twist, Riker takes the promotion. He and Deanna share an emotional farewell. It is a good scene.

Then he confronts his father as more tension mounts. They decide to settle their problems with an ambo-jitsu match. This disappoints me, but I figure the producers on high would grumble if there was all talk and no action, even if the talk presented good characterization.

Worf's friends set up The Age of Ascension ceremony. Data says the true test is to admit one's most profound feelings under pain of distress.

After Worf goes through the holographic pain stick line, he thanks his friends. This reminds me of the spanking scene in the film ANIMAL HOUSE when the kid says, "Thank you, sir, may I have another." I really did laugh, and I know it wasn't supposed to be funny.

In another bad scene, Deanna and Pulaski talk about men never growing up, sons always being children in their father's eyes, and father's expectations never ending. I don't see the difference between this and moms and daughters. Just look at Deanna's own situation with Lwaxana.

Riker and Kyle fight without vision. I couldn't figure out if they were using the Force or some other power to hit each other with their weapon sticks. Kyle cheats to win. Riker is furious when he finds out.

Riker thinks his father should have died instead of his mother, even though Riker was not very old when she died. We see the pain of the misunderstood father as Kyle confesses his love. We never learn how the mom died. Perhaps that's beside the point. At the end, Riker decides to stay on the Enterprise.

It's a weird episode.

EPISODE FORTY-ONE: "PEN PALS"

Teleplay by Melinda M. Snodgrass
From a story by Hannah Louise Shearer
Directed by Winrich Kolbe
Guest Cast: Nicholas Cascone, Nikki Cox, Ann H. Gillespie, Whitney Rydbeck

Throughout the series, Data explores the nature of humanity, occasionally involving non-human beings. On STAR TREK nearly everyone is humanoid; to be non-human means having extra fingers or a slightly misshapen face. Such is the case of the young girl Data communicates with here.

This is a touching episode. They invoke the Prime Directive when Data wants to save an alien child. Contact with off world societies would destroy normal cultural development. Data shows great humanity.

The Prime Directive is a rule. Data obeys rules, but he also knows how to question them and see their flaws and inconsistencies. He's better at this than Picard who often cloaks himself in the Prime Directive to avoid difficult moral decisions.

Data receives communication from a world ravaged by seismic disturbances. His plea to help the child and her people is supported by Dr. Pulaski and a reluctant Picard.

While the Enterprise works to save the planet from destruction, Data brings the child to the Enterprise for medical aid. Picard is unhappy, but allows Data and Dr. Pulaski to work things out. Data leaves a crystal with the child. It's an interesting touch. It seems that Data doesn't want the little girl to forget him, a very emotional response.

This episode avoids by-the-numbers storytelling and explores complicated issues common in Starfleet.

[ADDITIONAL COMMENTARY BY WENDY RATHBONE]

This is a very good story. It's believable when Wes solves a problem because he has a team to help him. This time, when Wes comes up with a solution to stabilize a world with intelligent life, it doesn't seem to grow out of thin air. His team of experts work with him.

A great story shows Wes learning to handle command. This episode also shows the great respect he has for Picard, though Picard often shows little warmth toward him.

The characterization is wonderful. Wes is nervous when he takes charge of the team. This illustrates how tensions arise. I commend the authors for this subplot. It offers true humanity aboard the Enterprise while staying away from the sterile atmosphere of the bridge.

Meanwhile, Data has his own project, the meat of the episode. Data hears a weak signal from a system much like the one the Enterprise is exploring. This system is also unstable. The computer translates the signal, which reads: "Is anyone out there?"

The message is from a young female alien named Sarjenka. Her world suffers from great geological upheavals. Picard tells Data to cease transmissions rather than violate the Prime Directive. There is a problem with this reaction from Picard. Not answering alien signals directed toward space contradicts their mission "to seek out new life."

The command crew debates the Prime Directive. Data points out that the Dramians, Sarjenka's people, are not a subject for philosophical debate but endangered people. The android says this rather than the human characters. Picard coldly points out that the Prime Directive is to protect themselves as well. He orders Data to end contact.

Data broadcasts the girl's voice before cutting it off so all in the room can hear her pathetic plea. She's dying. Now she is not a statistic, or a philosophical point, but a person. Picard can no longer turn his back. It is a ballistic scene. I didn't breathe all through this fine TV writing.

Picard is paid poor service by the writers. His behavior is rude, pretentious, snobbish, aloof and generally negative. He is not a person I would want to know.

Data materializes in the girl's room. The child runs into her room after her family has evacuated. She comes back for her transmitter, and finds Data. Then danger increases as the house shakes. Data makes a quick decision to beam up with the girl.

Another great scene follows, filled with tension and discovery. The thrill is dissipated by the coldness of the crew when Data brings the girl to the bridge. Picard has reason to be upset. Kids aren't allowed on his bridge! He immediately shows displeasure to Data. Picard and Riker show anger, tension and selfishness in front of a frightened alien child whose world is dying.

Sarjenka watches as a solution is found to save her dying world. It's a great scene, despite the unfriendliness of the crew.

Picard orders Pulaski to erase all the memories of Sarjenka's journey to the ship from the child's mind. If this is possible, why couldn't Picard be friendlier, knowing that she would never remember him? This is a fault in Picard. If the author's intent is to show that Picard is fallible, they did a good job. Picard is not a hero, Data is, and so is Sarjenka.

Picard is the anti-hero. He is the enemy against which Data must struggle to save the world. Picard's behavior adds strength to this story. Tension and character flaws lead to good storytelling.

Data shows compassion. He almost cracks a smile at the end. He shows more feeling than any of the rest of the crew.

I will think about this story over and over again. It raises question after question. You can debate the right and wrong of Data's and Picard's actions long after the credits roll. A very powerful story has been told. This episode shows character flaws and strengths in powerful, tension-ridden scenes, without one single starship chase or fight scene.

EPISODE FORTY-TWO: "Q WHO"

Written by Maurice Hurley
Directed by Rob Bowman
Guest Cast: John deLancie, Lycia Naff

The third appearance of Q finally effectively depicts the character. Q is still annoying, but no longer destructive. His actions sometimes appear bewildering, but a near omnipotent being would have a very different point of view. Other beings exist in a blink of an eye compared to his immortality.

Even immortals exercise whims. Q decides he wants to join Picard's crew without attending Starfleet Academy. He proves his worth, but Picard finds the entity too troublesome.

Q moves the Enterprise seven thousand light years, forcing Picard to ask for help to escape confrontation with a strange race known as the Borg. This episode introduced the Borg, later a major threat.

Q meets Guinan. They are old enemies who last met 200 years ago, although Q knew her by another name then. This is the first time we realize there is much we don't know about Guinan. She has no plans to let us in on those secrets.

This encounter will bring the Borg in search of the Federation. Early in the episode, a reference is made to the destruction of outposts in "The Neutral Zone" the previous year when a Borg scout ship entered Federation space.

Q's actions lead to a loss of life. Eighteen crew members die when the Borg slice a section out of the Enterprise for examination. The special effects are spectacular.

[ADDITIONAL COMMENTARY BY WENDY RATHBONE]

Q is back. Picard exits the turbolift and enters a shuttle far away from the Enterprise. Q is piloting.

I love the scene just before Picard enters the turbolift. New crewman Sonya Gomez bumps into the Captain, spilling hot chocolate all over him. Q cleans it with a swipe of his hand.

The new crewman, Sonya, is wonderful, a real person on a cardboard Enterprise. Even her hairstyle is down and wild. I approve.

Q and Picard appear in Ten-Forward. Surprisingly, Guinan and Q recognize each other. Q wants to join the crew of the Enterprise. He promises to renounce his powers. Picard refuses. An angry Q throws the Enterprise 7000 light years off course.

They are now in an unknown part of the galaxy, which Guinan recognizes. There are many ruined worlds. Guinan shows fear, and recommends they head home immediately. At warp nine it will take them two years.

They prepare to leave but encounter a Borg ship. Q wanted them to meet the Borg. Guinan explains that the Borg destroyed her home world, scattering survivors throughout the galaxy over 100 years ago.

I love the scenes with Guinan. She's an enigmatic, intriguing character. Actress Whoopi Goldberg gets credit for bringing vitality to what could have been a cold-hearted alien role.

The Borg ship fires on the Enterprise in a series of fantastic special effects. It carves up the starship. The Enterprise fights back, damaging over 20 percent of the Borg ship, proving they aren't invincible. Eighteen people die on the Enterprise during the attack.

I love the scene when Sonya tells Geordi that she can't stop thinking about the 18 deaths. This shows how human she is, and how new to the ship. Seasoned officers such as Geordi and Picard are trained not to show their feelings. That is often a disappointment to the viewing audiences.

Riker can't quite hide his own feelings. He accuses Q of being responsible for the deaths. Q seems unconcerned, though he assures them this is no illusion. He points out that this is the great unknown reality the Enterprise faces in its journeys. Q teaches a lesson to the puny, stupid officers by showing them this horror.

Data and Riker discover that the Borg share a hive mind, a biological and technological interface. They beam to the gigantic ship amidst awesome special effects. Riker, Data and Worf discover a nursery where Borgs are made. The babies are born "human" before being transformed. It is horrifying. The baby in Borg make up and costume is priceless.

The concept of the Borg is a good one. Mixing man and machine is an interesting theme, one that offers good story possibilities for future episodes.

Suspense mounts as the Borg ship fires on the Enterprise to destroy the shields. Picard finally admits he needs Q. Q then sends the ship back to where it started, away from the Borg. Q tells Picard that exploring the unknown is not for the timid.

This excellent episode offers many enigmas without resolving them with a pat little solution at the end. The Borg concept is ingenious. Whoopi Goldberg delivers an inspired performance as Guinan. Q is darkly charming.

I didn't think I would like Q, or the concept of a Q Continuum, when I first started watching the series. Now I think Q offers a lingering and intriguing threat for future episodes. Q is a hero when he helps the Federation by showing them the Borg in advance. Now they can prepare for this invasion.

There is a problem, though. If Guinan's people were destroyed by the Borg 100 years ago, why haven't they told anyone? The Borg are loose in the galaxy, wrecking havoc, and the survivors don't bother to mention it? That's a bit hard to believe.

This time the ideas are solid, the suspense is intense and the acting is top-notch.

EPISODE FORTY-THREE: "SAMARITAN SNARE"

Written by Robert L. McCullough
Directed by Les Landau
Guest Cast: Christopher Collins, Leslie Morris, Daniel Bemzau, Lycia Naff, Tzi Ma

The Enterprise encounters the Pakleds, a race that can't properly operate their own spacecraft. They kidnap Geordi for help. The Pakleds appear to be morons from outer space.

The "B" story features Captain Picard sharing a shuttle with Wesley. Picard heads for a medical exam while Wesley needs to take exams at the same starbase. Picard tells Wesley he has an artificial heart acquired after an ill-advised encounter with aliens when he was much younger. The encounter is more fully revealed in a later episode, "Tapestry."

This is the first mention of Picard's artificial heart. The captain fears people will treat him differently if they know. Dr. Pulaski gets a good scene at the end, but the producers still don't know what to do with her. They hadn't known what to do with Dr. Crusher, either.

[ADDITIONAL COMMENTARY BY WENDY RATHBONE]

Wes takes Starfleet Academy tests while Picard gets a new artificial heart. They travel together by shuttle craft to Starbase 515.

Meanwhile, new crewman Sonya Gomez adds spice to the Enterprise.

The second story features Riker commanding the ship while Picard is away. They receive a distress signal from a shipload of Pakleds, a race of scavengers who appear mentally deficient. Their mission is to "look for things" to "make us go."

These fat, slow-moving humanoids sent the distress signal for help fixing their ship. Riker offers assistance, and sends Geordi to do repairs. Deanna warns that the Pakleds are not helpless, and Geordi is in danger. Deanna doesn't belong on the bridge of the ship warning commanders of impending doom they never heed. Riker trusts his non-empathic eyes. The Pakleds look harmless, so he doesn't believe her. That is ridiculous behavior from a commander of a starship and a Starfleet officer. This is very bad writing of the character.

Deanna makes the next scenes predictable. I figured she wouldn't be wrong about her warning, so I knew the Pakleds would kidnap Geordi. I was not wrong.

They snatch his phaser, shoot him, then raise shields. They had hidden this technology from Riker. Now Riker cannot beam Geordi to safety. The suspense begins.

Dialogue between Wes and Picard on the shuttle is excellent. We learn about both characters, and discover that Picard has made mistakes in his wild youth. He is not the perfect man he tries to appear.

When they arrive at Starbase 515, the exterior shot shows a beautiful city on an Earth-like planet. It is a great matte painting.

I have many quibbles with this episode, but I liked the parts involving Wes and Picard. Picard was quite arrogant and irritating to Wes and Pulaski, a strength of the character. Even wonder boy Wes was cool in this episode.

EPISODE FORTY-FOUR: "UP THE LONG LADDER"

Written by Melinda M. Snodgrass
Directed by Winrich Kolbe
Guest Cast: Barrie Ingham, Jon deVries, Rosalyn Landor

[COMMENTARY BY WENDY RATHBONE]

The Enterprise saves a colony of humans, the Bringloidi, from their dying world. The humans came to the world in the 22nd Century, and now need to relocate. The 223 colonists beam up with their livestock because they won't leave their animals behind to die. Picard beams them to the cargo bays. He is very curt and impolite until someone sets a cooking fire, triggering the ship's safety systems. Then he finally laughs.

Pulaski and Worf share a Klingon tea ceremony. The tea is poisonous to humans, but Pulaski willingly participates, injecting herself with an antidote before drinking. Worf is deeply honored. It proves Pulaski is one tough character.

Later the ship travels along looking for a solution for the homeless colonists. They find a sister colony to the Bringloidi. They were split apart and the second colony crashed on a class M planet that looks like Saturn.

These colonists call their world Mariposa, the name of the ship of both groups of colonists, and the Spanish word for "butterfly." They are clones of the five scientists who crash landed.

When Pulaski and Riker discover this, they ask a lot of stupid questions. Pulaski asks about the clone sex drive. She asks why they don't create new variations in the children. When she asks about their sex drive, she really means to ask how they keep from reproducing.

Everyone but Pulaski knows you can have all kinds of sex without producing offspring. She asks because there is a flaw in clones that causes children to be weak, ensuring that their species will die out. The sex drive is purposefully inhibited.

I question this. There's also a flaw in cloning clones from clones called replicant-fading. There is no difference between producing a weak species through procreation or through cloning. Either way, society dies. Why inhibit the sex drive if it won't save them?

The cloning process in this episode is ridiculously amateurish. This story shows that clones are grown to adult form from both Pulaski's and Riker's DNA. They grow fast without becoming fetuses first.

The original scientists could have made unlimited clones of themselves. They only needed to freeze their bodies after they died. Their bodies could have been harvested for DNA. The clones are dying because they are cloning themselves from each other, which is very stupid.

The clone colony begs the Enterprise for fresh DNA to infuse their dying world. The Enterprise refuses because Riker feels it would diminish him as a human. He is as ignorant as Pulaski and the scientists who started it all! Would it diminish Riker to get a woman pregnant? I think not. Well, it's the same thing. This episode gets worse and worse.

The Mariposans steal DNA from Riker and Pulaski. When Riker and Pulaski discover this, they head straight for the vats and find themselves nearly full-grown. So Riker kills them. He kills innocent, growing life forms! I almost turned the TV off, but I kept it on to complete this review fairly.

The desperate, dying colonists cannot be helped. The Enterprise crew looks on them without compassion. Then they get a brilliant idea. The Bringloidi in the cargo bay need somewhere safe to colonize. They are the brothers of the original Mariposans. They move them to Mariposa to infuse the dying clone colony with human life. At first, the Mariposan clones are too snobbish to want them. Finally, they agree.

Pulaski tells the Bringloidi colonists that they cannot be monogamous if they are to survive. They must quickly populate the world. Each woman should have children by at least three different men. The woman who threw herself at Riker thinks about this, then decides there are worse fates.

Some women may not want to be baby factories. None of this is thought through in this sloppy episode. Nobody thinks that people would immigrate to Mariposa now that the Enterprise has found the lost colony. It will be on Federation maps. It's a beautiful Earth-like world. Who would not be tempted?

What if humans and aliens from other worlds set up shop there? What if the Ferengi decide they're ripe for trade? What's this nonsense about women having to have three husbands? I mean, it's fine if that's what they choose, but it's not at all necessary.

EPISODE FORTY-FIVE: "MANHUNT"
Written by Terry Devereaux
Directed by Rob Bowman
Guest Cast: Majel Barrett, Robert Costanzo, Rod Arrants, Carel Struycken, Robert O'Reilly, Rhonda Aldrich, Mick Fleetwood

This episode features the return of Dixon Hill and the annoying Lwaxana Troi. Picard uses the Dixon Hill program to hide from Deanna's mother, still portrayed as a good-natured, overbearing shrew. She's not very bright. When she follows Picard into the holodeck, he distracts her by introducing her to one of the holograms, which she engages in a long, spirited conversation.

Lwaxana uses her telepathic abilities in strange ways, such as when she casually reveals that two passengers are assassins. She needles Picard by announcing he has lustful fantasies about her, which we already know is not the case. The portrayal of Lwaxana is a bit pathetic, as though she's a lonely middle-aged woman forcing herself on people to find a relationship.

[ADDITIONAL COMMENTARY BY WENDY RATHBONE]
Much to Picard and Deanna's dismay, Lwaxana Troi comes on board as an ambassador. The humor is great, especially when she comments that Picard and Riker have nice legs when they are wearing their "dress" uniforms.

Riker learns that the Antideans, who boarded in suspended animation, are waking. He goes to the holodeck to tell Picard. Can't he just "beep" the captain? I don't think Picard would go anywhere on his own ship where he couldn't be contacted. Perhaps Riker uses this as an excuse to get away from Lwaxana.

Lwaxana and Mr. Homn follow Data and Riker into Picard's Dixon Hill fantasy. Lwaxana doesn't seem to understand that the holodeck people aren't real. She falls for Rex, the bartender.

Pulaski then "beeps" Picard from sickbay to say that the Antideans are on their feet. What's the big deal about the Antideans waking up? They were supposed to wake up.

Later Lwaxana is angry at being tricked into thinking Rex was a real person. She meets Picard and crew in the transporter room to beam down to the conference with the Antideans. She casually mentions that the Antideans are actually assassins wearing gowns lined with explosive devices. They plan to blow up the entire conference. Data confirms this after scanning them, and the Antideans are quickly taken into custody.

After all her foolishness, Lwaxana becomes the hero of the story. This is a great touch in an otherwise slow, very flawed episode. The humor works. I could do without the Dixon Hill stuff, though. It was boring, and felt like filler for a weak story.

Mick Fleetwood appears in this episode, though you wouldn't recognize him in his fish-eyed Antidean assassin make up.

EPISODE FORTY-SIX: "THE EMISSARY"

Television story and teleplay by Richard Manning and Hans Beimler
From a story by Thomas H. Calder
Directed by Cliff Bole
Guest Cast: Suzie Plakson, Lance LeGault, Georgann Johnson

This Klingon episode spotlights Worf and introduces K'Ehleyr, the half Klingon-half human mystery woman from Worf's past. She'll have a large impact on his future after she informs him that he's a father, several years after the fact.

When we first meet K'Ehleyr, we only know that Worf doesn't like her. We're surprised to discover that his enmity started when she turned down his marriage proposal. He felt dishonored. It's interesting to see them come to terms as she rejects the Klingon traditions which Worf treasures. They don't agree even when they reach a minimal understanding.

The primary and the secondary story center on Worf and K'Ehleyr. The Klingon Empire announces that records indicate that a Klingon vessel has been in a distant sector of space with its crew in suspended animation for 80 years. The ship began its trip before the Klingon-Federation armistice.

When the Enterprise encounters the ship, Worf and K'Ehleyr claim to be in command, indicating that the Klingon Empire defeated and absorbed the Federation.

K'Ehleyr is an excellent character.

[ADDITIONAL COMMENTARY BY WENDY RATHBONE]

A probe brings an envoy to the Enterprise, beginning a ridiculous plot. The Klingons made no provisions for a ship returning after an eighty year mission. No explanation is offered why this ship and crew have to be destroyed or what their mission discovered.

Deanna and K'Ehleyr play a very good character scene when they discuss being half-human.

Worf gets increasingly edgy, until Picard tells him to relax. Worf then replies, "I AM RELAXED!" It is a very humorous scene.

K'Ehleyr and Worf fight, then sniff each other to make up. While this may seem bizarre to Americans, it is actually a part of Southeast Asian culture. Until recent years, and the incursion of American movies, they didn't kiss. Instead they practiced what they smell each other. This involves burying your nose in the skin of your partner and sniffing vigorously. Many still prefer this to kissing. It's interesting that Klingons follow a similar practice. Perhaps one of the writers was familiar with Southeast Asian culture.

Worf claims they are mated. K'Ehleyr freaks out, saying she refuses to marry, or take the oath, with him. Worf appears very unappealing in this episode. He is pushy and selfish, and seems without empathy.

Afterwards, Riker asks Worf, "How did you like command?"

Worf replies, "Comfortable chair."

That's amusing.

There is a problem, though. When they beam K'Ehleyr over to take command of the T'Ong, the Klingons should notice that she's half-human. Some Klingon stories refer to human-fusion Klingons in the Empire. This could explain why they wouldn't be suspicious of her.

Suzie Plakson delivers an excellent portrayal as K'Ehleyr. She also played a Vulcan in the episode "The Schizoid Man." Plakson brought reality to what could have been a cliché Klingon female.

The excellent story idea could have been better executed. Inspired acting, especially by Plakson, improved the episode.

EPISODE FORTY-SEVEN: "PEAK PERFORMANCE"

Written by David Kemper
Directed by Robert Scheerer
Guest Cast: Roy Brocksmith, Armin Shimerman, David L. Lander

Another good story begins when Riker commands a frigate in war games against the Enterprise. It shows how Riker would fare in command of his own ship, the Hathaway, an eighty year old decommissioned vessel. Riker and his team restore it as best they can in 48 hours. His crew includes Worf, Wesley and Geordi.

Precocious Wesley brings a "science project" on board the Hathaway to allow the vessel two seconds of warp drive. It's quite a science project.

A subplot foreshadows events in season six's episode "Relics." A Ferengi ship happens on the war games and takes aggressive action. The Hathaway and the Enterprise, whose weapons have been neutralized for the war games, use trickery to drive off the Ferengi. Before this the Ferengi were not aggressive. One wonders what Starfleet did with this news. The Ferengi had been aggressive in "The Last Outpost" and "The Battle." In "Rascals," a Ferengi ship tried to steal the Enterprise.

Starfleet began a program of war games to prepare for the coming of the Borg. It reminds the audience of this storyline, although resolution still waited a year away.

EPISODE FORTY-EIGHT: "SHADES OF GRAY"
Teleplay by Maurice Hurley, Richard Manning and Hans Beimler
Story by Maurice Hurley
Directed by Rob Bowman

An indigenous life form stings Riker while he surveys an uncharted planet. He suffers flashbacks to scenes from earlier episodes. We suffer along with him.

He wakes up, but most in the audience remain asleep. What is there to say about an episode like this? Did the producers really think the audience would wonder if Will Riker was going to die? Did they think we wouldn't notice that this was all done as a cost-cutting measure?

Episodic films called serials appeared in the 1930s and '40s. One episode was shown each week at Saturday matinees in movie houses. Many serials recapped earlier chapters about halfway through. Characters sat around talking about what had happened until then as scenes from previous episodes appeared on the screen. It stretched low budgets and filled in new viewers. "Shades of Gray" did the same thing.

Making it the final episode of the second season was a silly idea. Season three began ending each season with a cliffhanger leading into the following season.

[ADDITIONAL COMMENTARY BY WENDY RATHBONE]
Riker is bit by something on an unknown alien world. His body begins to go numb. The bite injected organisms into his nervous system at the molecular level. The transporter cannot filter them out and Pulaski cannot surgically remove the organisms. She says that they will kill Riker.

Data and Geordi return to the planet to find what bit Riker. Pulaski will then be able to find a cure.

Picard visits Riker and seems to pretend concern. Either Patrick Stewart had a bad acting day, or the writers were up to something. The Enterprise sickbay is sterile and uncomfortable.

Deanna asks Riker, who at this point only has hours to live, why he jokes with the nurses. He shows no fear of death, and refuses to give up. Perhaps it is merely a brave facade. Otherwise this is a very boring character, or another case of bad writing.

A device is put on Riker's head to help stimulate the nerves in his brain and keep him from dying. Needles are inserted directly into his brain, causing Riker to suffer a series of bizarre, hallucinatory dreams.

Flashbacks arrive from the first two seasons, perhaps so the producers could save money on filming new scenes. While Riker suffers recollections, primarily of kissing women, Deanna feels some of what Riker feels. She tells Pulaski, and as they monitor the helpless Riker, they discuss his erotic emotions. It is very invasive of Riker's privacy.

Erotic memories attract the microbes, so Pulaski stimulates sad and angry memories. It's a bit like S&M, but it works. The bad memories repel the infection.

I question why the producers ran a flashback episode with only two seasons of the series under their belt. There's not enough depth yet to keep from being repetitive. Why couldn't they film new memories so the viewers could gain insight into Riker? Saving money is not a good enough excuse. This episode fails, and bores the viewer.

It is odd that basic negative emotions poison the organism. The organism preys on animals that constantly experience basic negative emotions.

The episode delivers zero suspense. The viewer knows they will cure Riker, so where's the intrigue?

SEASON

THREE

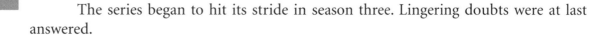

The series began to hit its stride in season three. Lingering doubts were at last answered.

[BY WENDY RATHBONE]

SEASON THREE

EPISODE FORTY-NINE: "EVOLUTION"

Teleplay by Michael Piller
Story by Michael Piller and Michael Wagner
Directed by Winrich Kolbe
Guest Cast: Ken Jenkins

The Enterprise, with an additional scientist aboard, investigates a stellar anomaly. They start to launch a probe called "the egg," but get pulled into the anomaly. The computer and other mechanical devices act strangely, but the computer refuses to acknowledge malfunctions. It senses a nonexistent Borg ship, mumbles chess moves and exhibits other bizarre behavior.

The malfunctions put the mission in jeopardy. The expert, Dr. Stubbs, would rather die than leave. His whole life is wrapped up in this project.

Early in the episode it is obvious that this arrogant, pompous zealot will cause problems, a standard cliché character and plot device. Starfleet appears well staffed with such people.

Wes caused the computer malfunctions with his science project. He altered two harmless nanites to allow them to learn. They escaped when he fell asleep. He believes they infiltrated the Enterprise systems, but doesn't believe the harmless nanites caused all the malfunctions. In an excellent scene, Guinan points out that Dr. Frankenstein thought the same thing.

Wes delays informing anyone of his suspicions. I don't understand why a youngster is trusted with potentially dangerous substances. The nanites must be contained, yet Wes allowed them to escape.

Wes finally confesses, after allowing the story time to build suspense. The crew learns about the evolved nanites. They mechanically replicate themselves. Crusher says they share a collective intelligence. It is remarkable that one kid's science project did all that.

Picard is not angry at Wes. They could all die, but there's no animosity. Usually Picard is not so patient.

They work together to remove the nanites without killing them. They want to study, not murder, the potentially new, sentient life form.

Dr. Stubbs only wants to get on with his project. He attacks the nanites, killing many. It's a big mistake. The nanites retaliate to protect themselves. First Wes, and now the zealot, put the Enterprise in mortal danger. Picard and crew worry that they've made an enemy of this new life form.

Then Data volunteers to act as a conduit to communicate with the nanites. No one comments on the potential danger. The nanites inhabit Data long enough to learn that the Enterprise crew wants peace. Dr. Stubbs apologizes, and peace begins.

Stubbs continues his experiment, with the nanites' help. The nanites continue evolving until they find the ship too confining. They then relocate to a world of their own!

I think Wes is now a god! He created new life in his science project. When the nanites get religion, will they seek Wes out as their god? Wouldn't that be a funny sequel.

EPISODE FIFTY: "THE ENSIGNS OF COMMAND"
Written by Melinda M. Snodgrass
Directed by Cliff Bole
Guest Cast: Eileen Seeley, Mark L. Taylor, Richard Allen

Data plays the violin while Dr. Crusher returns as if she'd never left.

A treaty gave the Sheliak a planetary system. They are obsessed with the letter of that treaty and believe themselves superior to humans. They don't respect human life, and refuse to negotiate with Picard about evacuating human colonists.

The colonist leader proves unwilling to leave. Data reasons with him, but he refuses to listen to a machine. This is a ridiculous plot complication, used when nothing better could be thought up.

A young woman befriends Data and kisses him. She wants to know if he can feel, and helps him test himself every chance she gets.

Data fails to convince the colonists of the threat. She suggests that Data use reverse psychology. He takes her advice to heart, but it too fails.

At first, when they failed to react, I guessed they weren't human but energy entities of some sort who could take care of themselves under the Sheliak threat. They are human, but just don't believe Data.

The leader shoots Data, fearing he threatens his authority. Of 15,000 colonists, we only see a few dozen. I'd like to know what the majority thought of Data's warning.

Picard and Deanna beam to the Sheliak ship, then walk down a corridor like the one that houses the Great and Powerful Oz. They continue to negotiate to no avail.

A repaired Data decides to destroy the colony aqueduct to show non-believers their weakness. Picard finally guesses that there might be a useful loophole in the 500,000 word treaty. Instead of the dozens of experts among the ship's passengers and crew that should be working on finding the loophole, Picard spots it himself. The hero finds that it allows third party arbitration in disputes between Federation and Sheliak people.

The Sheliak agree. Picard picks the Grisella race. They will remain in hibernation for another six months. He tells the Sheliak to wait six months before colonizing the world, or give them the three weeks they need. The Sheliak immediately grant them the three weeks.

This episode fails, but the parts with Data are endearing. The story provides a lesson in human behavior for Data. The theme is creativity. Data's creativity convinces the colonists of their danger while Picard solves the Sheliak problem.

EPISODE FIFTY-ONE: "THE SURVIVORS"

Written by Michael Wagner
Directed by Les Landau
Guest Cast: John Anderson, Anne Haney

This top-notch entry explores ideas new to STAR TREK. The Enterprise discovers two human survivors on a planet devastated by an alien attack. Their curiosity is heightened because the modest dwelling occupied by the two old folks is the only undamaged patch of ground on the planet.

The couple refuse to be evacuated. Finally the man reveals that he is of a species previously unknown to the Federation.

The alien had taken human form to marry a human woman when he'd fallen in love. Despite the massive powers of his people, his kind are pacifists. His wife chose to join the colonists fighting the alien attackers. She died with the others. Her husband struck out in his grief, destroying not only the attacking ship, but every last member of the race the ship represented throughout the universe!

John Anderson plays the heartsick, pacifist superbeing in a touching performance as he confesses to what he has done. He later created an illusion of his dead wife to keep him company in his now self-imposed exile.

The touching story by Michael Wagner has a rare downbeat ending. The race he represents has never been encountered again. The role was one of Anderson's last before he died a year later.

"The Survivors" began more location shooting for the series. It added immeasurably to the realism of the planet exteriors. Dark, turbulent worlds work on a sound stage, but Class M (earth-like) planets look better shot outdoors.

EPISODE FIFTY-TWO: "WHO WATCHES THE WATCHERS"

Written by Richard Manning and Hans Beimler
Directed by Robert Weimer
Guest Cast: Kathryn Leigh Scott, Ray Wise, James Greene, Pamela Segall, John McLiam, James McIntire, Lois Hall

The Enterprise assists repairs on a reactor at an outpost on the planet Mintaka. The outpost scientists study Mintakans, proto-Vulcanoids. The hologram disguising the outpost fades as their reactor fails. Two "bronze age" Mintakans see the outpost, violating the Prime Directive and interfering with their culture.

One is injured badly and taken to the ship for medical attention. He witnesses beaming, then wakens in sickbay. Captain Picard tells Crusher she should not have brought the Mintakan to the ship but left him to die. He doesn't even relent when Crusher tells him that they were responsible for the injuries and he had already seen the outpost through the windows. The writer made Picard a very unsympathetic character in this scene. He is hardly the hero of the series.

Crusher's attempts to erase the Mintakan's memories of the ship fail. The Mintakan tells his people of his religious experience, and that the "overseer's" name is "the Picard." It serves Picard right that he is now thought of as a god after being so cold.

The head scientist tells Picard that interference damage has already occurred, and Picard will do no more harm by revealing the truth. Picard finally acquiesces, and beams up the leader, Nuria, to show her their advanced technology. He shows her a dying scientist in sickbay, and tells her he has limits. This effective scene shows great compassion for a less advanced species.

Nuria returns to her people with Picard, and tells them of her religious experience. She shoots Picard to demonstrate his supernatural power. Picard is willing to sacrifice his life to prove he's not a god. He falls and bleeds, but recovers and tells the Mintakans they must find their own way. The writer ignores that the Mintakans will want to learn from the more advanced beings even if they aren't gods.

This is a weakness of the Prime Directive. People will not want to retain more primitive cultures when they learn of more advanced technologies. They shouldn't have to endure the same slow process and costly mistakes. More advanced civilizations should give them a helping hand.

EPISODE FIFTY-THREE: "THE BONDING"

Written by Ronald D. Moore
Directed by Winrich Kolbe
Guest Cast: Susan Powell, Gabriel Damon, Raymond D. Turner

The Enterprise explores ruins on an empty planet until an away team member is killed by an antique weapon. She is the only parent of a 12 year old boy, Jeremy Aster. Worf, the away team's leader, feels personally responsible; it's the first time he's lost a crew member under his command. Wes recalls how he felt when his own father died.

The excellent idea propelling this episode allows important discussions to occur. Picard gives a great speech to Troi about carrying children on board a starship. He feels it's wrong. This subject needed addressing long ago.

At first Jeremy appears to take the death of his mom quite calmly. Worf, out of guilt, demands the right to have a Klingon "bonding" ceremony with Jeremy. Their first meeting is very awkward, offering excellent character revelation.

The episode falls apart when they detect an energy source on the planet. The energy touches the Enterprise, and Jeremy's dead mother appears to him in his quarters. The entity-mom tells Jeremy they're going to live in a house on the planet below. Worf knows something is terribly wrong and reports the intruder. Picard and Troi pull Jeremy away from her as they try to beam down. The entity-mom vanishes, leaving behind a very upset Jeremy. He still doesn't say much, as if writers presume 12 year old boys are often tongue-tied. He is old enough to know that this wasn't his mom.

Jeremy's mom appears again, begging him to go with her. He doesn't resist, perhaps because grief makes him irrational. This is not a convincing scene.

The entity-mom energy being wants no more suffering from the "matter" beings' war that destroyed the planet. The energy beings feel it is their duty to make Jeremy happy again. In a lame scene, Picard explains that grief is a part of the life of mortal beings. Wes tells of his experience losing his father. The alien listens. Jeremy acknowledges feeling anger at Worf, and sorrow for his loss, but the expression of emotions seems contrived.

The alien understands this must be the way for humans, and leaves. The touching scene rings a bit false. It doesn't quite work. At the end, Jeremy "bonds" with Worf, becoming Worf's brother, a part of his family for all time.

This strong episode suffered from a weak ending. The energy beings on the planet seem too cliché. I would've preferred an honest episode about human grief. I heard that this episode originally involved the holodeck before it was rewritten to make the illusion an alien creation. I would have preferred the first idea, with little Jeremy conjuring his mother on the holodeck for comfort, then getting lost in the illusion.

EPISODE FIFTY-FOUR: "BOOBY TRAP"

Written by Ron Roman, Michael Pillar, Richard Danus and Michael Wagner
Directed by Gabrielle Beaumont
Guest Cast: Susan Gibney, Albert Hall, Julie Warner

The Enterprise answers the distress signal of a thousand year-old Promellian battle cruiser. Picard, Data and Worf beam over to explore it. One touching scene shows Picard thrilled to see the ships because he had a model of one in a bottle when he was a boy. Data and Worf don't understand his sentiments. Worf claims never to have played with toys, and Data was never a boy. Then O'Brien, at the transporter station, pipes up that he had ships in bottles when he was a boy.

It's a very funny scene. Riker gives him an accusing look, as if he suspects O'Brien of trying to please Picard.

Another priceless scene occurs when Geordi goes to Guinan for love advice. He's having trouble with his new love interest, Christy Henshaw. Guinan tells him he's trying too hard, and admits to being attracted to bald men. Picard comes immediately to mind, making the scene even more "telling."

As the Enterprise leaves the Promellian ship, they find themselves caught in an energy drop. The ship won't move. They have discovered the same ancient booby trap that caught the Promellian ship. When the shields fall, radiation will kill everyone aboard, just as it did the ancient Promellians of the 1000 year dead battle cruiser.

Tension in this scene is great as they only have three hours before the shields fail and they all die. Since there is no radiation left on the Promellian battlecruiser, perhaps they all could beam over to that ship to save themselves? The writers appear to have missed this possibility.

Geordi recreates the Enterprise engine designer, Dr. Leah Brahms, in a holodeck simulation to help him solve the problem. He even recreates simulated systems to test their theories. The ingenious Geordi ends up being the hero of the entire episode.

Unfortunately Geordi and Brahms exchange a lot of techno-babble and pseudo-science in place of dialogue. It quickly grows nonsensical. I'd rather the writers had showed how people on the ship reacted to impending death.

Geordi's solution requires turning all systems of the Enterprise over to the computer. Picard and Riker hesitate for no apparent reason, wasting precious time debating the issue. I also don't understand why Geordi doesn't have a team of engineers help with the problem. Only he and Brahms' hologram work on it. Does everyone else on the ship simply twiddle their thumbs and wait?

The solution seems improbably easy. If a trap uses your own power source against you, you simply turn your power off. It took them a long time to figure this out. I like the premise of this episode and the relationship Geordi has with Dr. Brahms' holo-simulation. She's a good character, if a little wooden.

The fairly good story offers unfortunately wooden emotional responses by the characters. Guinan rings true, and Geordi is excellent, but something is missing by not showing how other people on board the ship react to imminent death.

EPISODE FIFTY-FIVE: "THE ENEMY"
Written by David Kemper and Michael Piller
Directed by David Carson
Guest Cast: John Snyder, Andreas Katsulas, Steve Rankin

Geordi falls into a pit and is stranded on the stormy Galorndan Core after investigating a Romulan crash site. Riker and Worf fail to find him, but beam up a Romulan survivor.

Geordi struggles out of his pit only to run into a second Romulan survivor. Conflicts include the Enterprise running into a Romulan ship, and Dr. Crusher struggling to save the dying Romulan. She needs a substance found only in Worf's cells to heal him. Worf, a staunch enemy of the Romulans since he witnessed them kill his parents when he was a child, refuses to donate the needed substance.

This offers a wonderful plot conflict. Worf struggles with prejudice and guilt, and, surprisingly, is not talked into donating. The Romulan tells Worf he'd rather die than take anything from his stinking body. This hardens Worf's heart.

The Romulan dies in a strange twist for the usual happy ending. Worf must live with his actions. Questions remain. Did Worf get revenge? Does it make him feel good? Or does it make him feel empty? I wish this conflict had been dealt with further in the episode. The conflict between Geordi and the Romulan, Bochra, on the planet, is also handled well.

Geordi's VISOR malfunctions, leaving him blind. Bochra must be Geordi's eyes. Great special effects show what Geordi sees from his point of view through his malfunctioning VISOR. There are so many colors it's breathtaking. Forcing Geordi to rely on the Romulan to save them both is a good plot gimmick, particularly since the Romulan doesn't trust Geordi.

I like this episode. There is no happy ending for Crusher or Worf when the Romulan dies in sickbay, but Geordi plays hero and makes a new friend.

Andreas Katsulas plays the Romulan Commander, Tomalak. He now portrays a regular, Jakar, the Naren ambassador, on BABYLON 5.

EPISODE FIFTY-SIX: "THE PRICE"

Written by Hannah Louise Shearer
Directed Robert Scheerer
Guest Cast: Matt McCoy, Elizabeth Hoffman, Castulo Guerra, Scott Thomson, Dan Shor, Kevin Peter Hall

Deanna suffers from stress. She gets frustrated when the computer can't produce a "real" chocolate sundae for her. I like seeing the personal sides of the crew. This episode shows a very personal side of Deanna.

The story revolves around a wormhole near the Barzan planet. It is reputed to be the only stable wormhole ever discovered. This episode aired before DS9. It offers the first reference to quadrants of the galaxy labeled Delta and Gamma.

This wormhole allows ships quick passage into the Gamma quadrant, an area that normally takes 70 years to reach with 24th Century technology. Rights to the wormhole are being auctioned by the Barzans. The writers use this mechanism to introduce various delegations.

The Enterprise hosts the talks. Deanna meets, and falls madly in love with, one of the bidders, a human named Devinoni. At first I thought he was very forward with her. He comes onto her hard and fast, with little introduction. Later, we learn the empath, a one-quarter Betazoid, read her emotions, and knew exactly what she wanted.

A really great scene occurs when Devinoni oils Deanna's foot. Another great scene has Deanna and Dr. Crusher exercising together, and discussing the pros and cons of falling in love quickly. It is a wonderful, intimate conversation. STAR TREK presents too few of these scenes.

The Ferengi appear up to their usual tricks. They irritate me, but they create good, minor plot conflicts. Data and Geordi shuttle into the wormhole to run tests. They discover that it is not stable at the other end. Ships using it will be lost. The wormhole story is interesting, but the real story is of Deanna's love.

When she learns Devinoni is empathic, it raises questions about his character. The relationship forces him to take a better look at himself. The character grows in this episode. Those are the best kinds of stories to tell.

When characters learn from their actions, they become more real, and more sympathetic in the eyes of the viewer. At first I disliked Devinoni, but seeing him through Deanna's eyes helped me see other qualities. The episode surprised me when it turned out Devinoni assisted the Ferengi in their intrigue.

Marina Sirtis gives a good performance. Revealing the more personal lives of the Enterprise crew offers intriguing storytelling.

EPISODE FIFTY-SEVEN: "THE VENGEANCE FACTOR"
Written by Sam Rolfe
Directed by Timothy Bond
Guest Cast: Lisa Wilcox, Joey Aresco, Nancy Parsons, Stephen Lee, Mark Lawrence

The Enterprise crew beam down to a base to find chaos, and two injured humans. They theorize that The Gatherers, a race of nomadic aliens expelled 100 years before from their home world, are responsible. The crew makes solving the Gatherer problem a personal priority. They fly to Acamar III, the Gatherers' old homeworld, to talk the Acamarians into seeking a truce with the Gatherers and granting them immunity so they can return home.

Why do all this? The Gatherers are dangerous marauders. Who would want them? If the Gatherers are happy, why force this reunion?

The Enterprise crew persuade the Acamarian sovereign to sit down to "talks" with the Gatherers, but first they need some Gatherers. They find a Gatherer camp and get the leader to sit down and talk with the Acamar sovereign.

An assassin lies waiting among the Acamarians. The sweet, shy female servant of the Acamarian sovereign is a murderer, a product of the blood feud between clans. Her clan was supposedly wiped out. She's the last of her kind, and wants to kill the last of the clan that killed her clan. This weak subplot appears to have been added only because the main story wouldn't sustain an episode.

The Gatherers are all male. They all wear heavy leather and metal outfits that make it difficult to maneuver. They swagger. It is quite laughable, but fits a ridiculous story.

Riker falls for the traitor. He tries to draw her out of her shyness. We have already seen her kill, so we know his heart will be broken.

The crew decides that the traitor is Yuta, the servant. A plot error shows us too early that she is a murderer. It is then wasteful to show the crew solving the mystery. It is also anti-climactic.

Riker kills Yuta to stop her. This is a surprising major upset in the plot, but nothing is done with it. Riker shows no emotions.

Picard and Riker are so awkward with each other that Picard can't comfort him. Picard offers Riker shore leave, in a roundabout, awkward way.

This terrible episode offers no suspense or intrigue. Characters swagger and yell a lot. Events occur without emotional affect. Riker kills a woman he loves in an unusual surprise, illustrating that things in the Trek universe aren't always perfect.

EPISODE FIFTY-EIGHT: "THE DEFECTOR"

Written by Ronald D. Moore
Directed by Robert Scheerer
Guest Cast: James Sloyan, Andreas Katsulas, John Hancock, S.A. Templeman

I love the opening. Data practices dramatic acting by performing a scene from Shakespeare's "Henry V" on the holodeck. Picard is his acting coach. It is an excellent scene.

The Enterprise encounters a Romulan scout ship heading through the neutral zone, chased by a Romulan warbird. It desperately requests Federation aid. They beam the Romulan pilot aboard and take the ship in tow, rescuing him from his pursuer. The fleeing Romulan is a defector with vital information about a new secret Romulan base.

The Romulans plan a first strike against the Federation. Risk of damage to Federation outposts and colonies before help can come is very high. I like this idea. The enemy is a real person, not just a warrior bent on war and destruction or bigotry and hatred.

He seems sincere, especially when the Romulan warbird captain demands the defector's return. Then Geordi discovers that the warbird allowed the scout ship to escape, and they stop trusting the defector.

Picard acts as if he believes the claims of a base and new war. He cannot ignore the possibility. The crew prepares for war.

A great little scene occurs when Picard asks Data about crew morale. Data is surprised Picard doesn't know. Picard quotes from "Henry V," saying, "It's not easy for me to disguise myself and walk among my troops." He knows the crew act differently in his presence, and hopes Data can see their true side. It adds dimension and reality to this story.

Another interesting character scene leads nowhere, but is great writing. Data and Geordi discuss the relative values of fact and intuition. Geordi believes, in his gut, that the Romulan defector is telling the truth. Data wants to learn more about this "gut" response. It is an excellent aside.

I also like the dialogue between Data and the defector as he describes the beautiful world Romulus, and how he will never see it again because of what he's done to try to prevent another war. It's almost poetic. Data tries to recreate the world on the holodeck for the defector. A beautiful matte painting presents the image!

An excellent plot twist was not predictable. The defector is a Romulan admiral responsible for many massacres, but now he is being used by the Romulans. They fed him false information to test his loyalty knowing he would go to the Federation to try to prevent a war. The false facts would lure a starship into Romulan territory to give the appearance of a Federation first strike. The Romulans would then have an excuse to start another war.

Picard had not gone to investigate the base alone. Unknown to the viewer, he had cloaked Klingon allies with him. They uncloak and outnumber the Romulans, saving the Enterprise. It's very exciting when it happens. I never tire of seeing giant ships uncloak on a backdrop of black space and tiny stars. This episode is full of twists and turns, and does not end in a typical fashion of STAR TREK stories.

This great episode offers lots of characterization and plot twists and turns. One interesting bit adds a human side to the Romulans. The Romulan admiral has a daughter he wants to grow up safe without fear. It changed him from a cunning warrior to a pacifist.

The acting in this episode is above par. Even Picard manages to be likable.

EPISODE FIFTY-NINE: "THE HUNTED"
Written by Robin Bernheim
Directed by Cliff Bole
Guest Cast: Jeff McCarthy, James Cromwell

The Enterprise visits Angosia III, a world recovering from war. A dangerous prisoner escapes from the prison colony and the Enterprise aids in his capture. The prisoner, Roga Danar, is stronger than human. It takes five security men to detain him after he is beamed aboard.

Deanna senses the prisoner's nightmares and visits him in the brig. She learns he doesn't have an inherent violent personality. Researching his case she finds no criminal record. He served honorably during wartime. The hero volunteered to be biochemically and psychologically augmented as a soldier. Now, in peace, he and his comrades are obsolete and kept imprisoned so their irreversible programming will not endanger society.

This is a wonderful, Frankensteinian idea. The creature you create to save you finally turns on you. The Enterprise crew learns these "heroes" are brushed aside by their native society. The Angosians found it easier to exile the soldiers than to reintegrate them into society. This may be offered as interesting commentary on the difficulty some Vietnam War veterans had reintegrating into American society.

Ex-soldier Roga Danar's point of view is an interesting one. He is a lost soul who can't prevent his violent reactions and can never go home. They turn him over to Angosian authorities in a questionable action. Couldn't Roga Danar have asked for asylum?

Danar escapes and gives the security teams another good chase, even breaking out of a transporter beam. I've never seen that in any Trek episode before.

The chase is fun to watch at first, but it continues for too long. He eludes security and runs all over the ship.

The Angosians beg Picard for assistance. Picard refuses, using the non-interference directive as an excuse for not helping. It forces the Angosians to come to terms with their "soldiers" and try to live together in peace. Picard offers Federation assistance in helping psychologically treat the soldiers.

There is a problem with the logic of this episode. If the soldiers are so cunning and strong, how did the pacifist Angosians get them all rounded up and sent to Lunar V without another war? Wouldn't the soldiers have fought to keep from being jailed?

I like this idea. Beings created to help a society are later ostracized and feared when no longer needed. They were disposable people. I suspect Picard could have "interfered" when the people asked for his help, but he so disapproved of their treatment of war "heroes" that he used the Prime Directive to punish them. Picard manipulated events, a kind of interference.

EPISODE SIXTY: "THE HIGH GROUND"
Written by Melinda M. Snodgrass
Directed by Gabrielle Beaumont
Guest Cast: Kerrie Keene, Richard Cox, Marc Buckland, Fred. G. Smith, Christopher Pettiet

An Ansata terrorist kidnaps Dr. Crusher on Rutia. The terrorist needs a doctor, and wants to draw the Federation into his fight for autonomy. The terrorists use invertors to transport themselves without a trace. It involves interdimensional shifting that wrecks havoc with human DNA structures, eventually killing the people who use it. Crusher cannot save their lives, but only make them more comfortable as they die. The damage is already too severe.

The terrorist is depicted as a three-dimensional person, not just a bad guy with an agenda. The writer gave him an interesting personality. The terrorist is as adept at sketching as killing. He likes Crusher, and draws beautiful pictures of her. It shows his softer side.

This episode has its share of bloopers. The back of Wes' pants is undone when he, Data and Geordi attempt to discover how the terrorists travel. The terrorists do not take away Dr. Crusher's communication pin when they kidnap her. Couldn't she be traced through that? Picard also retains his pin after he is kidnapped.

Why do all the Rutian citizens wear purple? Is it a uniform in their society? The story never addresses this.

Data points out similarities to terrorists of Earth history. He tries to convince Picard that terrorism often works, referring to the Irish Unification of 2024. That's a great detail.

When the terrorists try to blow up the Enterprise, they lose my sympathy. They risk the lives of too many innocent people. Even their cause seems old and vague, perhaps reflecting similar situations in our current world.

This heavy-handed episode offers an over done lesson: "Maybe the end to violence begins with one boy putting down his gun." This is a bit too simplistic a solution. The terrorist problem on Rutia is solved when the headquarters are seized and people arrested. A "real" solution is never addressed. The annoying episode has some good moments.

EPISODE SIXTY-ONE: "DEJA Q"
Written by Richard Danus
Directed by Les Landau
Guest Cast: John deLancie, Corbin Bernsen, Richard Cansino, Betty Muramoto

A naked Q shows up on the bridge of the Enterprise claiming he has lost his powers. He seeks asylum from Picard. It appears that the Q Continuum kicked him out and gave him human form as punishment. Meanwhile, the ship helps people on a planet whose moon's orbit is deteriorating. It threatens all life on the world. The Enterprise desperately tries to move the moon back to its original orbit.

Q is amusing and interesting when reduced to human powers. He suffers from back pain, hunger, boredom and sleepiness.

The episode offers great dialogue when Picard requires proof from Q that he is not tricking them. Data and Troi verify his human readings. Worf thinks the best proof would be for Q to die. Then Q pipes back: "Have you eaten any good books lately?"

Guinan encounters Q in a good scene. She stabs him with a fork to prove to herself that he is human. (Well, it serves Q right.)

Q offers help with the moon dilemma. He suggests changing the gravitational constant of the universe so the moon will go back into correct orbit, without realizing Data and Geordi can't make the change.

Trouble comes when an intelligent life form composed of swirls of ionized gas probes the ship and finds Q. The life form, known as the Calamarain, wants revenge against Q. He has toyed with them much as he has with Picard and the Enterprise.

Picard wants to leave him at a starbase. Q wants to prove he's indispensable. Effective humor arises from the conflict. When the Calamarain attacks Q, the Enterprise raises her shields to protect him. It is not clear whether Picard operates on automatic pilot or really cares about Q.

The Enterprise never uses the universal translator to communicate with the Calamarain. This appears to be a flaw in story logic.

Q admits he is a coward, and hates being human. He steals a shuttle to turn himself over to the Calamarain and spare the Enterprise. Picard asks him to return. He even locks the transporter on Q to beam the shuttle back to the ship. Picard claims he doesn't want to lose a perfectly good shuttle, but there's obviously more to his motivations.

I felt empathy for Q. The imp has shown compassion. When he gets his powers back, he fixes the moon and gives Data the gift of laughter for a brief moment. Picard wonders if residue humanity remains in Q, but Q materializes a cigar in Picard's hand and says, "I don't think so."

A very human Q appears in a sympathetic light in this episode. Picard shows affection for the rude guy. Corbin Bernson delivers an inspired portrayal of the second Q. John de Lancie outdoes himself, also. This is a highly recommended episode with first rate humor.

EPISODE SIXTY-TWO: "A MATTER OF PERSPECTIVE"
Written by Ed Zuckerman
Directed by Cliff Boles
Guest Cast: Craig Richard Nelson, Gina Hecht, Mark Margolis

This episode opens with an excellent character bit. Picard takes a painting class, and Data critiques his work. Data dislikes Picard's style, making the captain squirm.

A dead scientist's widow and planetary security accuse Riker of murder. As Riker beamed off a science station, phaser fire from his direction hit a reactor, blowing up the station with Mr. Apgar on board. They hold a trial on the Enterprise, using the holodeck to recreate events according to witnesses. This isn't the Federation way, but the planetary government insists.

From Riker's point of view, the widow, Mrs. Apgar, threw herself at him. The scientist got upset and started a fight with Riker.

Mrs. Apgar's point of view shows Riker throwing himself at her as she resists his advances. In this scenario Riker forcibly kisses her.

Riker is upset at this portrayal of virtual attempted rape. Deanna can monitor if people are lying, and says that all are telling the truth as they see it. She also assures Riker that she believes his story.

Deanna appears a little too fair to Mrs. Apgar in this scene. The viewer knows Riker from previous episodes. It makes it obvious that Mrs. Apgar is lying to cover her actions. The writer should indicate that Deanna senses this.

Hearsay appears from the assistant to Dr. Apgar. In his view Apgar beat up Riker and Riker threatened him with death.

At this point, the episode becomes repetitive. Version after version appears of the same event.

As this takes place, radiation repeatedly appears on the ship, destroying indestructible metal. It is exactly the same type of Krieger waves Dr. Apgar was researching. It comes from the holodeck simulation. This makes no sense. Information about the science station was programmed into the holodeck simulation, but the facsimile can't recreate the Krieger waves. The anomaly helps Riker prove his innocence.

An interesting solution is offered to the murder mystery, but the episode is too low key and repetitive. It feels as if disinterested actors walked through this one like robots.

EPISODE SIXTY-THREE: "YESTERDAY'S ENTERPRISE"

Teleplay by Ira Steven Behr, Richard Manning, Hans Beimler and Ronald D. Moore.
From a story by Trent Christopher Ganing and Eric A. Stillwell
Directed by David Carson
Guest Cast: Denise Crosby, Christopher McDonald, Tricia O'Neil

This one offers a great teaser. Guinan gets Worf to drink prune juice. He calls it a "warrior's drink." It's a good touch, especially since Worf doesn't appear in the rest of the episode.

The story begins with a distortion altering the ship's time line. Everything changes. Tasha Yar is alive. The uniforms are different. No one but Guinan is aware of the difference.

Why is Guinan's species immune to the time-shift? It appears she's encountered the time-rift before. When she sees it out the 10-Forward porthole, she seems to recognize it.

The point of view of the story is not clear. The ship encounters an Enterprise from the past, making it appear that the story is told from the point of view of the past Enterprise. It is later clarified that the Enterprise-C is from 22 years in the past with a completely different crew and captain. The Enterprise-C is in trouble. At first, the Enterprise-D goes to help, but Picard doesn't want them to know who is helping.

Again Picard makes arbitrary decisions about interference. A ship is dying but he hesitates to help.

The Enterprise-C is commanded by a woman. The ship failed to save a Klingon colony, and somehow started a Klingon-Federation war that the current Enterprise is fighting. It explains why Worf is missing. Either he was never born, or his life was not saved in the Khitomer massacre.

Then a plot dilemma appears. They must send the Enterprise-C back to correct their time, but it is a death sentence. She will emerge at the time she left, in the middle of a battle with four Romulan birds of prey. Guinan insists they must go back but can't prove why.

The Enterprise-C captain agrees to go back. She makes a very calm decision to undertake a suicide mission. She knows they will die in battle.

Excellent characterization shows Yar feeling strange about herself and her place in the universe. She is drawn to Guinan and asks what happens to her in the other time line. Guinan's eyes tell that something is very wrong. Finally Guinan tells her they were never meant to meet.

Yar knows she can help if she transfers to the Enterprise-C, and that there's no point in staying in a future in which she will simply vanish. She requests a quick transfer from Picard.

The scene between Picard and Yar is cold and emotionless. They calmly sit talking about dying. The scene should have offered stronger emotion and angst. The relationship between Yar and the surviving Enterprise-C senior officer Richard Castillo is handled well.

A great climax sends the Enterprise-C back into the time rift as three Klingon battlecruisers appear. The Enterprise-D must now defend the Enterprise-C. The Enterprise-D suffers severe damage and Riker is killed. Many tragic events follow as a great plot device allows things that could never be done in a regular, linear time episode. The battle scene is very effective and suspenseful as the viewer knows anything can happen.

The Enterprise-C safely enters the rift, and everything immediately changes back to normal. Worf returns, the uniforms are restored and Riker is alive again. In a fantastic ending, Guinan sits down for a drink with Geordi and asks him to tell her about Yar.

This very powerful plot involves time-rifts and the past. It works well despite low-key emotional undertones.

EPISODE SIXTY-FOUR: "THE OFFSPRING"

Written by Rene Echeverria
Directed by Jonathan Frakes
Guest Cast: Hallie Todd, Nicolas Coster

Data secretly creates Lal (which means "beloved" in Hindi), a being with a positronic brain. When Lal is ready to be introduced, he tells the crew. The meddlesome Picard says he should have been consulted, but Data says others do not consult Picard about their procreation. Lal calls Data "father." Picard worries about Starfleet's reaction to this creation.

Data allows Lal to choose its own sex and appearance. It is a great idea. Lal chooses to appear as a human female. Wonderful scenes follow as Data teaches Lal. Lal differs from an ordinary child in an interesting way. She has an off switch; a handy device for the new parent.

Data even smiles in this episode! I'm not sure if this was in the script, or even intentional on the part of Brent Spiner, but it does happen.

Lal doesn't want to be different. It is difficult for her to accept.

A great plot complication arises when an admiral from Starfleet becomes interested in Lal. He wants to take her away from Data. This angers Picard, who has already once fought and won for Data's rights in "The Measure of a Man." Lal, he fears, is being seen as "property" and not an individual.

When Lal goes to work for Guinan at 10-Forward to learn about humans, she uses her first contraction: "I've." She surpasses Data in her ability to be human, learning about love and kissing. In an incredibly amusing scene, she kisses an unsuspecting Riker by lifting him up over the bar and planting one on his lips. Riker is quite shocked.

The admiral interviews Lal in a well-written scene. She proves she is more than a machine. The interview disturbs her as she feels something is very wrong.

She leaves the interview overwhelmed by fear, terrified of being taken away from her home and family on the Enterprise. It is heart-wrenching when she runs to Troi for assistance. Picard tries to help her.

The admiral argues with Picard, claiming that a starship is too unsafe for Lal. The ship is considered safe enough for civilians and children but not Lal? This makes little sense.

Lal malfunctions when she reaches full sentience. She suffers a breakdown. Data works hard to save her but fails. Her last words to Data are, "I love you, Father." This heart-breaking scene ends when Data absorbs her memories so he won't lose her completely. He carries her essence with him always.

The best NEXT GENERATION episodes involve Data and his rights as a machine being or Data and his attempts to learn humanity. I was close to tears when Lal died in one of the best episodes in the series.

EPISODE SIXTY-FIVE: "SINS OF THE FATHER"

Teleplay by Ronald D. Moore and W. Reed Moran
From a story by Drew Deighan
Directed by Les Landau
Guest Cast: Charles Cooper, Tony Todd, Patrick Massett, Thelma Lee

A Klingon warrior, Kurn, boards the Enterprise for assignment. He replaces Riker in a cultural exchange. He's tough on the crew except for Worf. This offends Worf, but Kurn talks down to Worf, as if Worf is inferior.

Worf confronts Kurn and learns Kurn is his younger brother. Kurn came to see if Worf is a true Klingon because it is the older brother who must challenge a charge against their dead father that he was a traitor at Khitomer. Picard offers to go with Worf to stand at his side at the trial. If the father is found to be a traitor, the entire family must pay for the crime.

A grim, pompous hearing follows. Their dead father has been accused of transmitting location codes to the Romulans. Little emotion is displayed in these boring scenes.

Pompous ceremony quickly bores the viewer. Worf chooses to accept discommendation to save the empire, as long as his brother is set free. He follows the most honorable course under the circumstances, although only K'mpec, Kurn, Duras, Picard and Worf know the truth. Discommendation demands that all Klingons turn away from Worf, including Kurn, whose identity remains secret. He was raised by a different family than his father's and can escape the condemnation.

Klingons in the Trek universe rarely behave in normal everyday fashion. This episode offers no more insight into Klingon nature or life. Instead it shows a trial based on ridiculous beliefs. The characters remain one-dimensional.

EPISODE SIXTY-SIX: "ALLEGIANCE"

Written by Richard Manning and Hans Beimler
Directed by Winrich Kolbe
Guest Cast: Steven Markle, Reiner Schone, Joycelyn O'Brien, Jerry Rector, Jeff Rector

Picard relaxes in his quarters until he is suddenly transported to an alien holding cell. He is imprisoned with a Mizarian and a Bolian Starfleet cadet. The crew thinks Picard is still on the ship because he was replaced with a replica. The replica Picard diverts the Enterprise from her mission with no explanation. He behaves subtly differently than the real Picard. The crew slowly realizes that something is wrong.

This is another tale of alien invasion and kidnapping. It is quite predictable. I quickly saw that this was a test because there was no other reason for the action. The four prisoners, the three were later joined by a fourth, each belong to a different race, belief system and profession. Picard knows of all their races so it seems to center on Picard.

Although I anticipated the typical plot, I was intrigued enough to keep watching.

In 10 Forward, Picard buys a round of ale for the house and toasts everyone with a song. This is not in character for Picard. His fellow officers suspect him, but Troi still senses nothing out of the ordinary. Since Picard is an alien, Troi should have detected the difference or some type of telepathic block.

Picard continues to put the Enterprise in danger. It appears to be a test of loyalty. How far will the crew blindly follow him? Everyone supports Riker when he relieves Picard of command. Picard offers little protest, proving he is not the true Picard. I like the subtle changes that clue the crew in. Little details are important, as is clear in Picard's behavior with the crew.

I also like the use of logic by the real Picard. He discovers that one of his fellow prisoners is the captor. Picard tests the Starfleet cadet with knowledge he has that she could not have. Her slip occurs long before Picard confronts her, and I puzzled why he waited. He knew the cadet wasn't whom she appeared to be, yet he continued to work with the others to find an escape.

When they finally open the cage door, a solid wall waits beyond. Picard tells the cadet he knows this is a test and refuses to play. He is immediately returned to the Enterprise. Two aliens follow to explain their actions. Picard reverses the tables, imprisoning the aliens in a stasis beam on the bridge. When they panic, he tells them that they now know how captivity feels. Then he releases them and orders them off his ship.

I like this episode. Picard taught the aliens a lesson. Then he ordered them off the ship. Yet isn't alien contact the Enterprise's chief mission? Shouldn't they have tried to establish more permanent communication?

The predictable episode offered good moments.

EPISODE SIXTY-SEVEN: "CAPTAIN'S HOLIDAY"

Written by Ira Steven Behr
Directed by Chip Chalmers
Guest Cast: Jennifer Hetrick, Karen Landry, Michael Champion, Max Grodenchik

This delightful, Indiana Jones-style episode begins when Picard is "forced" to take a vacation on the paradise world Risa. Picard's crew conspire to manipulate him into taking the vacation. Riker acts like a mother hen. Picard finally acquiesces to get away from the harassment. The scene works very well, presenting the characters in a human, humorous light.

Picard beams down directly into trouble. A futuristic device, the Tox Uthat, a pretty young woman, a Ferengi and alien Vogon time travelers from the 27th Century cause problems for the captain.

Before looking at the story, it's worth examining the humor in this episode. It is first rate. Riker tricks Picard by asking him to buy an artifact called a Horga'hn. Picard buys it, not knowing it is a symbol for sexuality. He sets it on a table near where he relaxes reading, and can't understand why women keep propositioning him. Then one woman explains that to display the device means he is seeking Jamaharon, something that is a mystery to Picard.

Picard tells the final woman he bought it for a friend. She asks, "Someone you love?" Irritated, he replies, "I wouldn't go that far." It looks as if Riker is in deep trouble when Picard gets back. I enjoyed a hearty laugh at that.

A Ferengi approaches Picard asking for a disk, but Picard knows nothing of a disk. Then a woman he first met when he beamed down approaches him. The woman, Vash, is embroiled in a search for the Tox Uthat. She slips a disk, the one the Ferengi searches for, into Picard's pocket. Picard is now involved. Vash and Picard search underground caves for the artifact.

Picard has a great time. He often calls up mysteries on the holodeck, so he is in his element. I was even wondering if this wasn't a set up planned by friends.

The Ferengi harasses Picard and Vash throughout the episode, even waving a weapon in public. Why would the vacation resort allow this?

I also question why Picard and Vash didn't have the Ferengi arrested before going to the caves. He's persistent. Didn't it occur to them that they might be followed?

Vash is a wonderful character. She perfectly matches Picard because they are so opposite in personality. Their first night conversation in the cave is wonderful. They are obviously drawn to each other. Instead of smarmy dialogue, they tease and have fun with each other. They match well when they become lovers. Vash challenges Picard out of his self-imposed shell.

I like this episode a lot, but the plot is silly. I love the character of Vash. She returned in later episodes. I also like the ending when Picard confronts Riker about the Horga'hn.

This great episode introduces a ballistic new love interest for Picard.

EPISODE SIXTY-EIGHT: "TIN MAN"

Written by Dennis Putman Bailey and David Bischoff
Directed by Robert Scheerer
Guest Cast: Harry Groener, Michael Cavanaugh, Peter Vogt, Colm Meaney

A new passenger delivers orders for the Enterprise. A former patient of Deanna Troi will be the mission specialist. Tam is a telepath of extraordinary power, and an expert at new alien contact.

The ship goes to contact a life form called the Tin Man that travels through space feeding on the wastes between stars. The creature has technological capabilities the Romulans want. They follow the Enterprise as it flies to meet Tin Man.

Several great character scenes appear in this episode, especially the one between Tam and Deanna. They discuss Tam's suffering and inner character. He was born telepathic on Betazed, where most children gain their telepathy in adolescence. Tam is considered a prodigy and an anomaly. His powerful telepathy nearly drives him insane because he can't shut out the thoughts of others, even over long distances.

The idea for this character is great. He can't interact with other people without appearing obnoxious or insane. Tam finally admits to Deanna that he knows Tin Man suffers in the same way he does. He is already in contact with it, although it is still light-years away. Tam is drawn to it. It has entered a system about to go nova because it wants to die.

The Enterprise battles Romulan ships who want the Tin Man. The story includes space battles to add tension and excitement, but they're not necessary.

A good scene shows Data's disappointment that Tam cannot read his mind. Tam tells him he can't read him because he is different, and being different is not a sin. This satisfies Data.

The ship comes upon Tin Man. It is a large, living starship. The Romulan ship partially disables the Enterprise, forcing it to travel slower to reach Tin Man. The Romulan ship has orders to destroy Tin Man if they can't have it. Tam contacts Tin Man, wakes it and tells it to defend itself.

Picard is suspicious of Tam's contact. Since Tam failed in a past mission when his partner was killed, Picard wonders if something is wrong with him. He might put the Enterprise in danger.

This part of the story is not handled well. The incident is not controversial enough for Starfleet to fire Tam, so why do Riker and Picard make more of it? Deanna trusts him. That should be enough.

A second Romulan ship tries to destroy Tin Man. Picard allows Tam to beam aboard the Tin Man. Effects for the interior of this alien creature are wonderful. It looks like a living being, except that there are corridors and tunnels. The creature's thoughts overwhelm Tam, but he loves it. It's the first time he's been free of distant thoughts. Now Tam and the star-creature no longer feel alone.

The second Romulan ship plans to fire, adding tension to the scene. At that moment, the sun goes nova and Tin Man throws the Enterprise and itself clear, saving them all. Then Tin Man returns Data to the bridge of the Enterprise, leaving Tam behind to stay with it forever.

This good episode is a little slow in parts. The characterization is excellent, but Riker and Picard's distrust of Tam looks contrived. The Romulan ships appear only to give the plot more tension. They also seem contrived.

EPISODE SIXTY-NINE: "HOLLOW PURSUITS"
Written by Sally Caves
Directed by Cliff Boles
Guest Cast: Dwight Schultz, Charley Lang, Colm Meaney

Lt. Reginald Barclay's holodeck pursuits are the opposite of his shy, insecure, stuttering personality. He is in trouble for being late and not giving "all" to his job. Behind his back, crew members refer to him as "Broccoli."

Good scripting and acting combine to present a great human personality in Barclay. This Enterprise crew member isn't perfect. He has faults and a penchant for daydreaming. This trait is common among STAR TREK fans.

The episode shows how Barclay interacts with the crew. He fantasizes an erotic image of Deanna that he often creates on the holodeck. His fantasies are cut short when things go wrong on the ship. Barclay must help solve the mystery.

It's hilarious when Picard slips and calls Barclay "Broccoli" in front of the bridge crew, especially since Picard prohibited the crew from using that nickname. He wanted to help Barclay. Picard's face turns redder and redder after the "slip."

Another wonderful scene involves a conversation between Guinan and Geordi. Geordi complains about Barclay's irritating habits, and about how Barclay just doesn't "fit in." Guinan replies, "The idea of fitting in just repels me." Wonderful! How often have we all felt that way?

A wonderful touch appears when Barclay makes his holodeck characters look like the Enterprise command crew. Sometimes the portrayals are not flattering. For example, Riker is much shorter in the holodeck image.

I don't understand why if Barclay has a very personal fantasy he wouldn't want others to see, he doesn't lock the holodeck door. If the doors don't lock, he could have programmed an alarm to automatically shut off the program. Instead the crew catch him "playing" with facsimiles of themselves.

At one point, Barclay says that the people on the holodeck are more real to him than the people outside. How many times have we felt that way when watching a favorite movie or TV show? Good writing often blurs the line between reality and fantasy.

More malfunctions occur on the ship, creating a life and death situation. As a fifteen minute deadline approaches, shy Barclay saves the ship in a tense scene. Barclay finally gets to be a hero off the holodeck. He discovers that real life can be as rewarding as escaping into fantasy.

This ingenious episode is a favorite of mine.

EPISODE SEVENTY: "THE MOST TOYS"
Written by Shari Goodhartz
Directed by Timothy Bond
Guest Cast: Jane Daly, Nehemiah Persoff, Saul Rubinek

Data shuttles supplies to a planet with a contaminated water supply. The crew sees the shuttle blow up. Before that, we see Data knocked out. The viewer is left to wonder whether he was on the shuttle. The Enterprise crew thinks they have just seen Data destroyed.

Data was actually kidnapped by Kivas Fajo. Fajo acts like a little kid with a toy. He tells Data he collects very rare items. Everything he has is one of a kind. Data is the crown jewel.

Data tries to escape. He looks for weaknesses in Fajo's assistant.

An excellent plot point appears when the crew figures out that the water contamination was actually sabotage. They suspect the person that gave them the decontaminant, Fajo, and pull up the records about him.

The computer informs them he is a collector of rare artifacts. Now Geordi suspects that the shuttle explosion was rigged, and Fajo has Data. This is too convenient. The plot falls apart.

I have problems with this episode. The Enterprise crew didn't know Fajo until late in the story. Fajo, his assistant, and Data wear terrible, unflattering costumes. The story idea is a good one, and seeing Data react as he does at the end, almost killing Fajo, is wonderful. Brent Spiner's acting is superb.

EPISODE SEVENTY-ONE: "SAREK"
Television story and teleplay by Peter S. Beagle
From a story by Mark Cushman and Jake Jacobs
Directed by Les Landau
Guest Cast: Mark Lenard, Joanna Miles, William Denis, Rocco Sisto

Spock's daddy, Sarek, played by Mark Lenard, boards the Enterprise. He behaves irritably for a Vulcan. Picard says Sarek is 202 years old. Perhaps Vulcans don't age gracefully.

Perrin, Sarek's wife, is arranging flowers when Picard asks her and Sarek to a Mozart concert. The writers thus establish that traditional arts and philosophies will survive into the 24th Century.

The 20th Century offers an interesting insight. Many people throughout the world have begun to revive the traditions of their culture, even in places where it had been thought lost. Large high tech skyscrapers in modern Hong Kong, for example, are constructed only after consulting an expert on earth force lines, or fengsui. They choose the placement of furniture and even the direction the building faces. International diamond merchants in New York City form a minyan and davit every morning, an ancient Jewish religious tradition. Flower arrangement, like the tea ceremony, has very significant philosophical meaning and deeply enhances the quality of life. The arrangements will be found in modern condominiums and computer installations throughout Asia, and as far afield as San Francisco.

This episode shows some passion, unlike too many others. The usually unflappable Sarek sheds an unVulcan tear at the Mozart concert. It startles everyone.

Heated, uncharacteristic arguments follow on the ship. Soon, there are all-out brawls everywhere. It almost seems to be a replay of "Day of the Dove." A negative entity may be taking over. No reason is found. The crew theorize that Sarek has Bendii Syndrome; a loss of mental control for Vulcans. The rare disease hits some Vulcans over the age of 200. It allows suppressed emotions to emerge. Sarek projects telepathically at random.

Picard suffers from Sarek's intense regrets, anguish and despair. Patrick Stewart delivers a fantastic performance.

This is an excellent episode. The overall impact is what Trek should be: exciting and emotional, with real conflicts overcome by real people. TV doesn't get much better than this.

EPISODE SEVENTY-TWO: "MÉNAGE À TROI"

Written by Fred Bronson and Susan Sackett
Directed by Robert Legato
Guest Cast: Majel Barrett, Frank Corsentino, Ethan Phillips, Peter Slutsker, Rudolph Willrich, Carel Struycken

Ferengi board the Enterprise to attend a reception to end a trade conference. Weird music at the party doesn't coincide with the finger strokes of the alien playing the instrument. Deanna and Lwaxana continue their familiar mother-daughter tensions. A Ferengi seems attracted to Lwaxana and determines to have her.

The episode makes clear that Betazoids cannot read Ferengi minds. It is a good plot detail.

I like this episode. Although I dislike the Ferengi plot device, I like Lwaxana. I did not like this character earlier in the series, but she has grown on me. She's a lot of fun.

Wes solves too many mysteries. He too often sees things the others miss. This could be the writers' self indulgence in what has become a cliché.

Susan Sackett, one of the writers of this episode, was Gene Roddenberry's assistant for many years. She's written books, including THE MAKING OF STAR TREK: THE MOTION PICTURE and STAR TREK SPEAKS as well as LETTERS FROM STAR TREK.

Director Rob Legato is also the TNG visual effects supervisor.

I like many things in this episode, including the humor, the tension between Deanna and Lwaxana, Wes' promotion and the look on Mr. Homn's face when he comes back from picking uttaberries to find the picnic spot abandoned. The characters still feel emotionally distant, though. This episode falls short.

EPISODE SEVENTY-THREE: "TRANSFIGURATIONS"

Written by Rene Echevarria
Directed by Tom Benko
Guest Cast: Mark Lamura, Charles Dennis, Julie Warner

The crew find an alien life pod on a rocky planet. The life pod gives off humanoid readings showing that the occupant is in critical condition. Crusher uses a device connected to Geordi's brain waves to beam the victim up to sickbay. I have not seen this done before. It's a good idea.

When Geordi is connected to the injured alien, there is an energy surge. Geordi seems unaffected.

I suspected something sinister had happened to Geordi. Then the story went in an entirely different, more positive, direction. The episode shows that Geordi has lost some of his youthful personal insecurities. He is more confident in his interactions with other people, especially a woman named Christy. This is a very well-done, subtle sub-plot.

Geordi and Data exchange far too much techno-babble as they figure out the origin of John Doe. This is the type of scene Gene Roddenberry never wanted. You do not halt action to describe how a device works. Here it's part of solving the mystery, but it goes on for too long. The computer diagrams that accompany the techno-babble must have taken days to create and shoot. The studio wasted a lot of time and money to get Data and Geordi to play pseudo-scientists in a scene that makes viewers yawn.

There's rapport between Crusher and John Doe. His physical contact with her while she operated may have made her a better, more sensitive doctor. The "healing" touch of John Doe is a permanent improvement, but it's not really addressed in the episode. John Doe helped everyone he came in contact with.

Eventually the Enterprise encounters an alien Zalconian ship, John Doe's people. They say John Doe is a criminal and want him returned. Then they give a two hour ultimatum.

It is not clear why they allow two hours instead of demanding immediate delivery. It gives the Enterprise time to decide what to do.

This is good Trek, although, at times, convenient, lazy plotting gets in the way. It has a positive theme: the enhancement of a species for the good of all. It shows goodness prospering over evil and even delivers a happy ending. This one is a winner.

EPISODE SEVENTY-FOUR: "THE BEST OF BOTH WORLDS"
Part One
Written by Michael Piller
Directed by Cliff Bole
Guest Cast: Elizabeth Dennehy, George Murdock

Providence Colony disappeared. The Enterprise suspects the Borg. Riker refuses a promotion to the Melbourne. It's a busy episode.

It's even poker night. I love poker nights on the Enterprise. There are two new players this time, Wes and Commander Shelby. Riker bluffs, but Shelby calls him on it, and wins a considerable pot. Poker shows a human side to the crew, which appears too infrequently in early seasons.

Deanna calls Riker "seasoned," referring to his reluctance to leave the Enterprise for a promotion. He doesn't like that word much. It's a good little scene.

The Enterprise learns that the Borg are involved and move to encounter them. I had a question while watching this. Why they want to deliberately provoke the Borg is unclear since they know they cannot win. Help is six days away. The writers conveniently forget they have civilians on board. The logical course would be to run and plan strategy, but Enterprise commanders always rely more on luck.

They first find an unidentified alien vessel. Picard, before learning it is the Borg, gives an order to intercept. Why he would do so without information is unclear. Engaging the Borg so quickly makes even less sense. I'm confused by this bad writing.

The special effects are very effective, though. The Borg ship is a cube with a rough, wiry surface.

Tension between Shelby and Riker enhances the story. She cuts Riker down to size with excellent lines, including, "If you're not prepared to make big decisions, step aside," and, "No wonder you've been standing around in the shadow of people like Picard." She implies that Riker is a weak, flimsy thing with no backbone.

Guinan, the best character on this show, is a survivor of a Borg attack on her homeworld. She reassures Picard in a great scene! I wish Guinan was in more episodes.

The Borg ship is dark, and full of wires, machines and cables. The beings who run the ship chose Picard as the human voice for them as they indoctrinate themselves into all human cultures. It could spell the end for Picard, creating good suspense.

The sound effects are creepy. The Borg ship sounds like a heavy breather. Air rushes through, along with the echoing hum of machinery. It is very stylistic. It is interesting that humans can board the Borg ship and walk around unmolested.

The episode ends on a cliffhanger as Riker gives the order to fire. It's not much of a cliffhanger, since we know they can hardly beat the Borg, even with Shelby's great ideas.

The Borg-bots are augmented men, part human and part machine. Picard makes for an interesting Borg, and doesn't have any hair to get in the way of the devices sucking on his brain.

The Enterprise attacks the Borg on its own, acting as if it must save the galaxy solo or die trying with civilians on board. This is a major flaw in the series. Civilians on the ship really hinder things.

Suspense builds effectively with Picard in danger. It makes the audience very nervous, but the flaws keep it from being a perfect episode.

SEASON

FOUR

It was full speed ahead with some of the best STAR TREK yet. New ideas and new alien threats appeared, promising an intriguing future.

[BY WENDY RATHBONE]

SEASON FOUR

EPISODE SEVENTY-FIVE: "THE BEST OF BOTH WORLDS"
Part Two
Written by Michael Piller
Directed by Cliff Bole
Guest Cast: Elizabeth Dennehy, George Murdock

The Enterprise can't possibly defeat the Borg. That doesn't stop them from trying.

The Enterprise was damaged at the end of part one. They arrive too late to help the armada fight the Borg at Wolf 359, the last stand before the Earth.

I like the shot of Picard getting a probe in the mechanism on the side of his head. All the color drains from his face. The special effects for this are very good.

In an excellent scene, Guinan pays a visit to Riker, and the viewer learns just how close they are. Her pep talk is forced, though. She says that the Borg now know everything Picard knows, so Riker has to do something unpredictable to defeat them. He has to do something Picard wouldn't consider.

Three murdered starship hulks float around Wolf 359. One ship, the Melbourne, is the ship Riker refused to command in part one. It adds a nice touch.

Taking a ship into battle with civilians aboard is nonsense. The Enterprise should dump the civilians then return if needed. Writers seem to forget them and write scripts as if the Enterprise is a warship and nothing more.

I like Riker's plan to beam Worf and Data to the Borg ship from a shuttle craft. I do question how the Enterprise implements successful attacks when an entire armada could not.

Through Picard, Data plugs into the systems that control the Borg. Suspense builds quickly. The Borg have reached the Earth and plan to infiltrate humanity.

Wes remains unbelievably calm. He hesitates to follow an order once, but it would have been more realistic if the camera had shown his hands shaking when he steered the ship into a suicide attack.

I don't understand the need for a self-destruct sequence on the Borg ship. I have a major problem with the series of suicide attacks while the Enterprise survived by the seat of its pants. Sometimes Riker doesn't even plan his attacks. This is unforgivable in a commander.

EPISODE SEVENTY-SIX: "FAMILY"

Written by Ronald D. Moore
Directed by Les Landau
Guest Cast: Jeremy Kemp, Samantha Eggar, Theodore Bikel, Georgia Brown, Dennis Creaghan

This story presents a rare example of television science fiction realistically following the consequences of a previous episode. This follow-up to "The Best of Both Worlds" tells of the less spectacular side-effects of the battle with the Borg.

Jean-Luc Picard chooses to take a well-earned shore leave on Earth. He returns to his home in France for the first time in twenty years. Picard struggles with psychological scars by returning home to his brother. Unresolved conflicts remain, but Jean-Luc wants to confront them. His older brother, Robert, is a farmer working to keep family traditions alive. Robert regards Jean-Luc as arrogant and ambitious. Jean-Luc's young nephew, Rene, remarks that Jean-Luc doesn't look arrogant.

The portrayal of Robert Picard is strange because he acts like a 20th Century man. It seems that life in the 24th Century would be so different from life today that no one would recall these "simpler" times. They would reflect back on more recent history. This part of Robert Picard's character does not ring true. It can be overlooked in light of more important issues. Jean-Luc's old friend Louis remarks that Jean-Luc has always reached for the future while Robert reached for the past.

Jean-Luc sees himself as a boy reflected in Rene. The child fixes his eyes firmly on the stars. Robert has to come to terms with a son who will follow in his uncle's footsteps, not his father's. The motion picture STAR TREK: GENERATIONS revealed that fate had something altogether different in store for Robert and Rene.

This is one of the best episodes NEXT GENERATION has produced. It bravely deals with human issues rather than galactic conflict. We understand these people and how each affects the other.

Two subplots fill out the episode. One involves Worf's human foster parents visiting the Enterprise. The other tells of Wesley watching a hologram of his father for the first time. It was made at the time of the boy's birth. The subplots distract from the infinitely more interesting main story of Jean-Luc coming to grips with his personal demons and reconciling with his brother.

Supposedly this episode did poorly in the ratings. It is one of their top ten entries in quality. It should have been nominated for the Humanities Award, the annual prize given to television writing that promotes strong human values. Perhaps if had it dealt only with Picard and dispensed with the padding of the minor subplots it would have received more serious consideration.

The actor who played Rene returned two years later to play Captain Picard when he's turned into a child in the sixth season episode "Rascals."

EPISODE SEVENTY-SEVEN: "BROTHERS"

Written by Rick Berman
Directed by Rob Bowman
Guest Cast: Cory Danzinger, Adam Ryen, James Lashly

Apparently the producers of NEXT GENERATION didn't like Lore any better than most viewers did. "Data's evil twin" first appeared in episode #13, then disappeared for three years. Dr. Soong, Data's creator, returns as well.

In a tour de force performance, Brent Spiner played the roles of Data, Lore and Dr. Soong. Actually anyone could have played the aged scientist under the tons of make-up. Performing three roles in one story is quite a hat trick, but it wasn't necessary.

Dr. Soong summons Data who then steals the Enterprise to go to the isolated world where the scientist waits. The android performs many tricks, including duplicating Picard's voice. He would make a dangerous foe. Although unspoken, it demonstrates the danger Lore could pose since he has no conscience.

Dr. Soong appears to be a kindly scientist who has developed an emotion chip for Data. Data gets it only after he defeats Lore in season seven. He doesn't install it in himself until STAR TREK: GENERATIONS.

EPISODE SEVENTY-EIGHT: "SUDDENLY HUMAN"

Teleplay by John Whelpley and Jeri Taylor
Story by Ralph Phillips
Directed by Gabrielle Beaumont
Guest Cast: Sherman Howard, Chad Allen, Barbara Townsend

At first this appears to be a story about child abuse. Even the coming attractions seem to say so. It's nothing of the sort.

It is more a story about how child abuse can be assumed when it's not really there. Even that turns out to be a secondary story element. It's really about displacement, loss and what is best for a child who grew up among the people who were responsible for the death of his parents.

Picard discovers that a human child, played by Chad Allen, has been raised by the aliens who killed the boy's family eleven years before. The captain decides to return the boy to his people, but the boy has become integrated into the alien culture. It is all that he knows.

Picard draws forth the boy's human memories, but finally realizes that he belongs with the foster father who loved and raised him. The child was five when his kidnappers began raising him. They have been good parents.

The episode raises difficult questions and provides uncomfortable answers. The original STAR TREK never took such a downbeat position. It shows the risks NEXT GENERATION is willing to take.

This story demonstrates that Earth born ethics may not always be appropriate for all worlds. The boy is clearly happy with his adopted people. His foster father is a good man. Twentieth Century morality may demand that the boy be returned to his human relatives, including a Starfleet officer, but this story adopts a 24th Century point of view.

The incident somewhat parallels actual events in the American West of the Nineteenth Century when Indians sometimes slaughtered settlers and kidnapped the children. The children raised among the Indians often did not want to return to the White world when given the opportunity.

EPISODE SEVENTY-NINE: "REMEMBER ME"

Written by Lee Sheldon
Directed by Cliff Bole
Guest Cast: Eric Menyuk, Bill Erwin

This episode plays with reality showing similarity to the books of author Philip K. Dick. When Dr. Crusher realizes that people she knows have disappeared from the Enterprise, she finds it difficult to convince anyone else. No trace of the missing people remains. It takes half the story before we realize what's happening. The pace sustains itself well.

The scenes when Dr. Crusher discovers people missing play with one's mind as the viewer tries to figure out the possibilities. Few will guess the solution. It involves Trek-speak and fantasy science stretched to the inexplicable, an interesting idea for one of the most unusual episodes.

Suspense and interest hinge completely on figuring out the truth. It will be much less interesting as a rerun. This story is very linear, with one plotline and no subplot distractions. It makes the story more effective.

EPISODE EIGHTY: "LEGACY"

Written by Joe Menosky
Directed by Robert Scheerer
Guest Cast: Beth Toussaint, Don Mirault

Tasha Yar lasted one season. She wasn't around long enough to reveal much background. All that was known is that she came from a failed Federation colony where civilization broke down and the people splintered into primitive warring factions, including roving bands of rapists.

The Enterprise stops over at the world where Tasha grew up when an orbiting Federation freighter sends out a distress signal. The only survivor aboard the freighter is Tasha Yar's sister. Ishara Yar is quickly accepted by Tasha's friends, the Enterprise crew members. It is well handled, particularly when Ishara betrays her new friends to try to destroy the opposing revolutionary faction.

It's a good story. There is a glitch, though. It establishes that Tasha left fifteen years before and that her sister had already joined the rebellion. Unfortunately, the actress playing Tasha's sister looks to be in her late twenties. It's hard to believe Tasha would abandon a 13 to 15 year old sister when she left the planet. This is never adequately explained although it is quite obvious.

One wonders why Starfleet didn't move in and fix this failed colony rather than allow it to continue as an embarrassment to the reputation of the Federation. Starfleet has more armament than either local faction. They could easily establish a provisional government, declare an amnesty and end the war.

Little is shown of this disintegrated colony. They never explain how things got so bad. Had Denise Crosby remained with the series, perhaps an episode would have delved into the background. This episode turns into routine instead. It could have been more memorable.

EPISODE EIGHTY-ONE: "REUNION"

Teleplay by Thomas Perry and Jo Perry &
Ronald D. Moore and Brandon Braga
From a story by Drew Deighan and Thomas Perry and Jo Perry
Directed by Jonathan Frakes
Guest Cast: Suzie Plakson, Robert O'Reilly, Patrick Massett, Charles Cooper, Jon Steuer, Michael Rider, April Grace, Basil Wallace, Mirron Edward Willis

The second season episode "The Emissary" confronted Worf with his old flame, K'Ehleyr. Worf meets K'Ehleyr again. This time she has news of great interest.

Their first encounter produced a son, Alexander. K'Ehleyr now wants to take the marriage vows she earlier declined. This time Worf doesn't want to follow through because of the Discommendation he accepted in season three. Worf doesn't want to bring disgrace on her.

This episode continues the tradition of focusing on Worf to explore his Klingon character and heritage. These episodes are consistently among the finest in the series. Picard is dragged in when the Klingon ritual of ascendancy to the Klingon throne is at hand. The subterfuge behind the scenes tells the tale.

Worf loses his mate but fights to the death with the man who killed her and caused Worf's Discommendation. Picard opposes Worf fighting to the death for any reason.

Worf's Klingon principles over-ride his Starfleet responsibilities. Picard doesn't punish Worf harshly as Worf had strong reason to do what he did. It's good to see Worf acting like a real Klingon rather than a tame Starfleet officer.

At the end Worf allows his adoptive parents to raise his son. It is touching and leaves opportunities for future stories. This episode marked the beginning of the "domesticating" of the Worf.

There is some question why Worf's son has a human name. Although never discussed, I suspect it is because the boy's half human mother, K'Ehleyr, rejected her Klingon heritage. She probably refused to give her child a Klingon name.

K'Ehleyr dies in this episode for no good reason. Fans still complain about the loss of a fascinating character.

EPISODE EIGHTY-TWO: "FUTURE IMPERFECT"

Written by J. Larry Carroll and David Bennett Carren
Directed by Les Landau
Guest Cast: Andreas Katsulas, Chris Demetral, Carolyn McCormick, Patti Yasutake, Todd Merrill, April Grace, George O'Hanlon, Jr.

This story plays with the nature of reality. It keeps us guessing right up to the end. Even as we congratulate ourselves for figuring out that Riker is being tricked by a Romulan illusion, we fail to realize it is an illusion within an illusion. The well-told tale holds up on repeated viewing even though we know what comes next.

Characterization and little details add weight to the underlying premise. Surprise is not all the story has to offer.

For much of the episode, Riker believes that sixteen years have passed and a long dormant virus has made him forget the intervening years. While we don't believe that, it's interesting to see what his "life" became in those years, including having a son named Jean-Luc and a wife, Minuet. Long time fans picked up on this discrepancy and congratulated themselves when Riker announced there never was a real Minuet. She was a hologram he met years before in the first season episode "11001001."

When the Romulans appear, we're sure we've got it figured out. Boy are we in for a surprise! Stories showing possible futures are always fascinating. This is one of the best.

It would be interesting science fiction even without the STAR TREK characters. Someone adapted a great idea for a science fiction story to the STAR TREK milieu creating one of the top 25 NEXT GENERATION episodes.

EPISODE EIGHTY-THREE: "FINAL MISSION"

Teleplay by Kacey Arnold-Ince and Jeri Taylor
Story by Kacey Arnold-Ince
Directed by Corey Allen
Guest Cast: Nick Tate, Kim Hamilton, Mary Kohnert

This is the episode many NEXT GENERATION fans prayed for since the first season. It marked the departure of Wil Wheaton as a series regular. Wesley Crusher had been cleansed of the sins of the first season, but still failed to fit in. He is not missed.

Wesley was Gene Roddenberry's favorite character. He worked hard to make him work, but it always seemed forced. Every time Wesley faced death, many viewers hoped Picard would fail to pull the kid's fat out of the fire.

The actor left the series to attend college and pursue film projects. Wil Wheaton made three films after he left the series. They flopped, one never getting a national theatrical release at all. Another, a made for TV movie shown on cable, received less than a stellar acceptance.

Wesley left to attend Starfleet Academy. This story focuses on him as he's given a fine send-off. We see many sides of his character when he's marooned on a small planet with Picard, along with the gruff captain of a mining shuttle. Although Wesley saves Picard in the end, he doesn't make it look easy. It will come as quite a surprise in season five when Wesley makes a guest appearance only to get his comeuppance!

Not many people know Wil Wheaton worked for a computer graphics company for a year, then approached Paramount about returning to NEXT GENERATION full time in 1993. Some producers supported this while others did not. Wesley Crusher made one last appearance in season seven and Rick Berman stated that there were no plans to include him in the NEXT GENERATION feature films. The young actor could only have regarded this as a slap in the face.

EPISODE EIGHTY-FOUR: "THE LOSS"
Teleplay by Hilary J. Bader and Alan J. Adler and Vanessa Greene
Story by Hilary J. Bader
Directed by Chip Chalmers
Guest Cast: Kim Braden, Mary Kohnert

This valiant attempt crafts an episode around Deanna Troi. Female characters on NEXT GENERATION consistently come in a distant second behind male stars of the show. Episodes focusing on Troi or Crusher were quite rare. When they did happen, they often seemed perfunctory and lacked narrative drive.

This episode traps the Enterprise inside a sentient particle cluster. It drags the ship towards a cosmic string fragment, causing Troi to lose her emphatic abilities. She wants to resign as ship's counselor. When she realizes she doesn't need her Betazoid abilities to dispense sound advice to people in trouble, she regains her self-esteem.

The crisis is averted and Troi gets her powers back. She now knows that her role as ship's counselor is not defined by her powers, but merely enhanced by them.

This is a very tame story. The best Troi episode, "Face of the Enemy," appeared in season six. It was written exactly the same way as it would have been for one of the male co-stars.

EPISODE EIGHTY-FIVE: "DATA'S DAY"
Teleplay by Harold Apter and Ronald D. Moore
Story by Harold Apter

Directed by Robert Wiemer
Guest Cast: Rosalind Chao, Sierra Pecheur, Alan Scarfe

Data sends Commander Maddox a letter describing a typical day aboard the Enterprise to help him understand life as an android. On this particular day, Data stands in for the father of the bride in the wedding of Keiko to Chief O'Brien. It's not a typical day.

The wedding becomes the usual subplot. The characters get cold feet and almost cancel the wedding until Data dispenses sound advice for the bride and groom.

Dr. Crusher gives Data dancing lessons, as actress Gates McFadden is a professional dancer as well as an actress. This episode also introduces Data's pet cat, Spot.

The other subplot of this episode involves a Vulcan ambassador, T'Pel, scheduled to be taken by the Enterprise to meet with a Romulan ambassador. When T'Pel is seemingly killed in a transporter accident while beaming to the Romulan ship, it leads to an espionage plot being exposed. It turns into a Data episode as well as a Romulan episode, taking the usual twists and turns of any story involving the Romulans.

If this is a typical day aboard the Enterprise, it's no wonder this flagship of Starfleet is so famous.

EPISODE EIGHTY-SIX: "THE WOUNDED"

Teleplay by Jeri Taylor
Story by Stuart Charno, Sara Charno and Cy Chernak
Directed by Chip Chalmers
Guest Cast: Bob Gunton, Rosalind Chao, Mark Alaimo, Marco Rodriguez, Time Winters, John Hancock

This crucial episode introduces the Cardassians to the STAR TREK universe. They are as nasty as the Klingons of the original STAR TREK, and more ruthless than the Romulans. The Cardassians are the kind of relentless, stereotyped villains Roddenberry later regretted creating. Roddenberry felt guilty about portraying an entire race as evil. He laid down new rules for THE NEXT GENERATION, making the Klingons a more interesting race of characters.

Starship captain Ben Maxwell is convinced that the Cardassians are preparing for war and decides to attack first, without consulting Starfleet. He had lost his entire immediate family to the Cardassians in the previous war and refuses to stand by and allow them to launch another campaign of terror.

The interesting story gives Miles O'Brien a good scene since he served with Maxwell in the past and fought the Cardassians in the war. O'Brien reveals that he killed Cardassians in the war and witnessed the aftermath of the slaughter at the colony where Captain Maxwell's family died.

There is an effective twist ending. Picard figures out that Maxwell had guessed correctly about the Cardassians. It is a nice touch. Maxwell's mistake was launching a counteroffensive without sufficient proof, and against Starfleet orders.

The Cardassians form a vital background element for DEEP SPACE NINE. Their one-note villainy was broadened in an episode of DEEP SPACE NINE titled "Duet." It features a Cardassian who tries to force his people to confront their collective guilt for war crimes.

EPISODE EIGHTY-SEVEN: "DEVIL'S DUE"

Teleplay by Philip Lazebenik
Story by Philip Lazebenik and William Douglas Lansford
Directed by Tom Benko
Guest Cast: Marta Dubois, Paul Lambert, Marcelo Tubert, William Glover, Thad Lamey, Tom Magee

A famous quotation from Arthur C. Clarke says, "Any sufficiently advanced technology is indistinguishable from magic." That premise forms the basis for this story.

One thousand years ago, the people of Ventax Two supposedly struck an accord with a being known as Ardra, their mythological version of the Devil. This agreement called for Ardra to guarantee a thousand years of harmony in the Ventax society. At the end of that time Ardra would return to claim the planet and its riches as her own. The 24th Century marks the end of the millennium. A woman calling herself Ardra appears on Ventax Two, demonstrating incredible powers. She says she's come to collect the debt.

One might question why an advanced society would believe that a demon of legend from a thousand years ago would still exist, but that isn't explored. The society is portrayed as superstitious. There is still a copy of the thousand year old contract that Data wants to study.

Picard thinks Ardra is a fraud even though the Ventaxians believe in her. The earth tremors she causes help prove her case, but the starship captain knows what 24th Century technology can do. The story is logical. Picard exposes Ardra and turns the tables on her.

What happens here could be perpetrated on other worlds. A con artist could use modern technology to extract wealth from a less advanced industrial society.

"Devil's Due" represents a headache that Starfleet must deal with on a regular basis. The galaxy is vast and space flight is available to many individuals.

EPISODE EIGHTY-EIGHT: "CLUES"

Teleplay by Bruce D. Arthurs and Joe Menosky
Story by Bruce D. Arthurs
Directed by Les Landau
Guest Cast: Pamela Winslow, Rhonda Aldrich, Patti Yasutake, Thomas Knickerbocker

The Enterprise crew have encountered aliens previously unknown to them, such as the omnipotent being in the third season episode "The Survivors." This episode concerns an encounter with xenophobic aliens distrustful of outsiders and willing to destroy anyone who discovers them.

The Enterprise detects a Class-M planet with a nearby wormhole-like energy fluctuation. Everyone on board except Data falls to the floor unconscious when the ship enters the wormhole. The crew regains consciousness and finds that the wormhole moved them one day's distance from their previous location in a matter of seconds. Then crew members discover that a day has passed, not mere seconds. What happened to the missing time?

The mystery deepens when Captain Picard suspects that Data knows more than he is saying. The android could pose a danger to them. Picard decides to return to the point from which they began, despite Data's objections.

The revelation of the mystery is a clever one that I doubt anyone could guess.

EPISODE EIGHTY-NINE: "FIRST CONTACT"

Teleplay by Dennis Russell Bailey, David Bischoff, Joe Menosky, Ronald D. Moore and Michael Piller
From a story by Marc Scott Zicree
Directed by Cliff Bole
Guest Cast: George Coe, Carolyn Seymour, George Hearn, Michael Ensign, Steven Anderson, Sachi Parker, Bebe Neuwirth

Riker is injured on the surface of a planet in a freak accident while disguised as an alien. He is exposed when taken to a hospital. The resulting paranoia regarding an "alien invasion" threatens his life.

A woman wants to accompany Picard back to the Enterprise when Riker is rescued. An official is terrified by the existence of the Enterprise. He distrusts beings from another world who possess power and technology superior to their own.

These events are kept from the public, but shock waves rage through a government previously unaware of life on other worlds. The wise and understanding ruler recognizes that their society is not equipped to deal with the sudden knowledge of alien worlds and futuristic technology.

The original STAR TREK never approached the idea of first contact in this complicated a fashion. This story is diminished somewhat by the Bebe Neuwirth character who wants to "have sex with an alien." The rest of the story takes the high road and demonstrates the drama of ideas.

The climax deals head on with how the Federation and the Prime Directive effect such a situation. This planet is very close to the point in development when the Federation makes contact, but they aren't quite ready. Picard agrees with the Chancellor. The Federation doesn't want to throw a society into disorder with a dose of future shock.

The scientist thrilled with discovering what awaits her people in space is allowed to live on the Enterprise. It will enable her to one day lead them to their future.

This episode is packed with thrilling ideas. It directly explores the notion of avoiding contact with societies not prepared to confront the reality of life on other worlds and demonstrates the necessity of the Prime Directive.

EPISODE NINETY: "GALAXY'S CHILD"

Teleplay by Maurice Hurley
Story by Thomas Kartozian
Directed by Winrich Kolbe
Guest Cast: Susan Gibney, Lanei Chapman, Jana Marie Hupp, April Grace

Aliens play a large part in STAR TREK, but they have usually been humanoid. Science fiction is most interesting when it presents non-humanoid aliens. The episode "Tin Man" is an example of that.

The Enterprise encounters a space faring whale. It attacks the Enterprise until it is accidentally killed by low level phaser fire. The starship becomes the foster mother to the child the creature spontaneously gives birth to. They must keep the baby alive until they find the rest of its kind.

That is the title story. The human story shows the Enterprise taking on a passenger, Dr. Leah Brahms. Geordi LaForge "met" her holographic projection in "Booby Trap." He consulted the hologram for help with the Enterprise engines. When the real Dr. Brahms discovers the hologram projection, she assumes Geordi did something kinky.

Dr. Brahms seems cold and unyielding, but, predictably, she and Geordi become friends. The "A" and "B" stories are only peripherally connected. Geordi and Dr. Brahms collaborate on a way to wean the alien off of the Enterprise so that it will join a herd of its own species.

This good episode depends on telling a solid story rather than engaging in outer space melodrama.

EPISODE NINETY-ONE: "NIGHT TERRORS"

Teleplay by Pamela Douglas and Jeri Taylor
Story by Shari Goodhartz
Directed by Les Landau
Guest Cast: Rosalind Chao, John Vickery, Duke Moosekian, Craig Hurley, Brian Tochi, Lanei Chapman, Deborah Taylor

This Troi episode depends largely on a dream sequence and a mystery that fails to provide the viewer with enough clues.

Crew members experience hallucinations and bouts of paranoia. None dream except Deanna. The Enterprise is trapped in a spacial rift. An unseen vessel of unknown origin is trapped on the other side. It tries to communicate telepathically with the Enterprise, but instead blocks out dreams. Deanna still dreams because she's a Betazoid.

Troi runs around acting distressed, but little happens. It could be argued that Troi and Data save the Enterprise. It's a strange and not very satisfying episode, largely because it seems padded to fill the hour.

EPISODE NINETY-TWO: "IDENTITY CRISIS"

Teleplay by Brannon Braga
Story by Timothy De Haas
Directed by Winrich Kolbe
Guest Cast: Maryann Plunkett, Patti Yasutake, Amick Byram, Dennis Madalone, Mona Grudt

This episode tells of an away team mission Geordi served on five years before on the USS Victory. The members of that away team investigated the disappearance of the staff of a Federation outpost. They have begun disappearing. He teams up with Susannah, the only remaining member of that away team, to discover what is happening.

The Enterprise finds mysteries, including alien footprints and tattered Starfleet uniforms, at the base. Something happened to the away team five years ago that is now causing them to transform into another species.

The episode uses ultraviolet light effects also effectively employed in STAR TREK VI: THE UNDISCOVERED COUNTRY. When Geordi undergoes the transformation, he looks unlike anything we've seen before.

The climax depends on the transformed Geordi, who still retains some of his humanity. He responds to Susannah, who had been cured of the infectious parasite. One reason Geordi may respond to her is that she's a woman. LaForge has problems with women paying attention to him. When one appeals to him, Geordi must respond.

EPISODE NINETY-THREE: "THE Nth DEGREE"

Written by Joe Menosky
Directed by Robert Legato
Guest Cast: Dwight Schultz, Jim Norton, Kay E. Kuter, Saxon Trainor, Page Leong, David Coburn

The earlier episode "Hollow Pursuits" introduced Reginald Barclay, played by Dwight Schultz. He's not your usual Enterprise crewman. Ordinarily a crewman is portrayed as perfect in every way, often lacking personality as a result. Barclay isn't perfect. Although highly intelligent, he has low self esteem. One wonders how he passed the Starfleet psychology tests since he seems to be a breeding ground for neurosis.

In the earlier appearance he was caught using the holo deck to create simulations of his superior officers whom he'd talk back to since he was too timorous to do so in reality. This time Barclay is taking lessons in self-confidence by studying acting.

When the Enterprise encounters an alien probe, it affects Barclay by boosting his intelligence. The shrinking violet soon becomes a mental giant. An alien race, the Cytherians, use this method to bring other entities to them. Barclay's IQ boost is only temporary.

Barclay is such an interesting character it's surprising the series didn't introduce more ordinary people. While the regulars aren't all portrayed as extraordinary, they lack human flaws. At worst Geordi is shy around women while Dr. Crusher is dull, but that's not quirky or eccentric. The original series tried harder to make their characters fallible humans.

EPISODE NINETY-FOUR: "QPID"

Teleplay by Ira Steven Behr
Story by Randee Russell and Ira Steven Behr
Directed by Cliff Bole
Guest Cast: Jennifer Hetrick, Clive Revill, John deLancie, Joi Staton

The Enterprise hosts an archeology symposium while orbiting Tagus 3. It is disrupted when Q appears and creates a Robin Hood scenario. Sadly, this episode returns to the annoying, silly Q from the first season.

Before Q arrived, Picard was reunited with Vash, the young woman from the planet Risa in the episode "Captain's Holiday." A nice scene occurs when Deanna Troi comes to see Captain Picard early in the morning and finds Vash in Jean-Luc's quarters. It implies that Vash spent the night.

Picard is a very private man. He's never told his friends about Vash. She thinks Picard is ashamed of her. He explains that he is a very private person, but she refuses to see it that way. Some women would have felt embarrassed if Picard had talked about them, and might have accused him of bragging about their affair. It just goes to show, you can't win.

Then Q turns up and uses his powers to create a Robin Hood scenario. Picard has to rescue Vash. Vash is so furious with Picard that she keeps thwarting him. This impresses Q. At the end, Vash decides to go off with Q, much to Picard's chagrin. Q was trying to do a good turn after all, not just being deliberately mischievous.

The Robin Hood storyline is silly. The relationship between Vash and Q doesn't last long. Their breakup appears in an early episode of DEEP SPACE NINE.

EPISODE NINETY-FIVE: "THE DRUMHEAD"

Written by Jeri Taylor
Directed by Jonathan Frakes

Guest Cast: Jean Simmons, Bruce French, Spence Garrett, Henry Woronicz, Earl Billings, Anne Shea

J'Dan, a Klingon exchange officer, is caught accessing security codes. When the Romulans obtain secret information concerning the dilithium chambers, J'Dan is believed to be the spy. Starfleet launches an immediate investigation.

This important episode plays with interesting ideas. A Federation official sees spies everywhere. He is prepared to convict innocent people to protect the Federation. Jean Simmons portrays Admiral Satie, the retired Federation officer sent to supervise the investigation.

It demonstrates that the Federation isn't squeaky clean. On the other hand, Picard shuts down the investigation before it harms innocent people. The system does work, and contains checks and balances.

Picard ends this investigation by demonstrating that Admiral Satie is paranoid. The admiral accuses him of violating the Prime Directive nine times while in command of the Enterprise, and even questions how he allowed a Romulan spy, disguised as a Vulcan, to escape. She even reminds Picard that while a captive of the Borg, he aided in the destruction of 39 Federation ships. It's a wonder Picard didn't go for her throat when she said that. This man shows self-control.

There was a spy aboard the Enterprise, a Klingon working for the Romulans. The incident is exaggerated until conspiracies are seen where none exist. Like "Measure of a Man" in season two, this shows that Starfleet can go too far in the pursuit of its goals. This story only impugns this particular admiral. It's a compelling tale that offers an interesting war of words.

EPISODE NINETY-SIX: "HALF A LIFE"
Teleplay by Peter Allen Fields
Story by Ted Roberts and Peter Allen Fields
Directed by Les Landau
Guest Cast: David Ogden Stiers, Majel Barrett, Michelle Forbes, Terrence M. McNally, Carel Struycken

One either finds Lwaxana Troi, as played by Majel Barrett, amusing or obnoxious. Until her appearance in "Half A Life," the character wasn't interesting. Cartoon characterization was abandoned in this episode when she falls in love with a man honor bound by his society to commit ritual suicide when he reaches the age of mandatory retirement. Refusal would bring horrible dishonor on his family.

This episode makes odd use of the Prime Directive. Picard feels he cannot interfere with the planet's culture. The Prime Directive only applies to planets not in the Federation. It deals with cultural pollution and interference with a society's natural development.

Kaelon-2, a member planet of the Federation, employs cruel and unusual cultural practices. Forcing productive members of a society to commit suicide at age 60 is not the natural development of a society. If a society slaughtered children, because families were not allowed more than two, it would not be considered natural.

This story addresses putting the old out to pasture when they still have much to contribute to society. On Earth this is practiced in subtle ways, particularly in Hollywood. That may have been one undertone of the story.

Majel Barrett is so good in this episode that one wonders why she tolerated having her character written as a cartoon before this. She is capable of depth and feeling and nary a joke passes her lips. The ending, when she agrees to take part in the final family gathering with Timicin, is touching and disturbing.

David Ogden Stiers plays Dr. Timicin. He is best known for his role as Major Charles Emerson Winchester on the last several years of the television series M*A*S*H. He does well in dramatic roles, but usually turns up in supporting parts rather than as a major featured player such as he is in this episode.

EPISODE NINETY-SEVEN: "THE HOST"

Written by Michel Horvat
Directed by Marvin V. Rush
Guest Cast: Franc Luz as Odan, Barbara Tarbuck, Nicole Orth-Pallavicini, William Newman, Patti Yasutake, Robert Harper

This episode introduces an element crucial to DEEP SPACE NINE. A Trill appears for the first time. The alien can enter and merge with a host body.

When this Trill's host body is injured, it temporarily relocates into Riker. Dr. Crusher had an affair with Odan, the Trill, in its previous host body. She didn't know Odan was a Trill, hardly the basis for an honest relationship.

Odan temporarily transferred into Riker while awaiting his new host body. Dr. Crusher continues her affair uninterrupted since Riker's consciousness is submerged while the Trill is present.

Or so the episode claims. In later stories on DEEP SPACE NINE, it explicitly states that the Trill merges with the host body and doesn't submerge the consciousness.

The ending caused controversy. The Trill's new permanent host body is female. Dr. Crusher breaks off the affair, saying too much is happening in too short a time for her to deal with it. She didn't have that objection when the Trill occupied Riker's body. Perhaps Dr. Crusher couldn't make love to a woman, although the producers deny this.

EPISODE NINETY-EIGHT: "THE MIND'S EYE"

Teleplay by Rene Echevarria
Story by Ken Schafer and Rene Echevarria
Directed by David Livingston

Guest Cast: Larry Dobkin, John Fleck, Edward Wiley, Denise Crosby (Majel Barrett receives screen credit as the voice of the computer for the first time in the history of the series.)

Romulans are an unusual race. NEXT GENERATION portrayed them as villains, but eventually established an armed truce and an exchange of intelligence. This was best exemplified in the third season of DEEP SPACE NINE when the Romulans lent the Federation a cloaking device.

In season four the Romulans were still bent on conquest with the Federation in their way, having formed a powerful alliance with the Klingon Empire. The Romulans broke off diplomatic relations with the Klingon Empire when it made peace with the Federation. Subsequent episodes revealed that the Romulans conspired with factions in the Klingon Empire. The Romulans massacred a Klingon outpost at Khitomer and earned the eternal enmity of the Empire.

Divide and conquer is an old idea. The Romulans kidnap Geordi and brainwash him as an instrument of assassination. If a Federation officer killed an important Klingon official, it could lead to the shattering of the alliance. The Romulans also try to make it look as if the Federation is arming Klingon rebels.

A Klingon is part of the conspiracy. When he's exposed, he pleads with Picard for asylum. Picard says he will grant asylum after the Klingons interrogate him. Considering the high price Klingon traitors pay, it's a wonder there are any. Being part of a rogue political faction is one thing, but consorting with Romulans in an assassination conspiracy is quite another.

This episode features a Romulan seen only in shadow. Her identity will eventually be revealed as Sela, the Romulan double for Tasha Yar. This revelation will occur in episode #100.

EPISODE NINETY-NINE: "IN THEORY"
Written by Joe Menosky and Ronald D. Moore
Directed by Patrick Stewart
Guest Cast: Michele Scarabelli, Rosalind Chao, Pamela Winslow

Data enters into a relationship with a young woman to try to understand romance; Jenna agrees because she's just come out of a bad relationship and doesn't want to be hurt again. It's obvious that she finds an android lacking human emotions interesting. He's relatively incapable of doing the inexplicable things human beings are sometimes capable of. For instance, he wouldn't say things to hurt her because he's incapable of using emotions as a tool.

The subplot tells of the Enterprise's encounter with "dark matter." It causes gaps in normal space. Picard pilots a shuttle to lead the Enterprise through the "dark matter." It is odd since Captain Picard isn't allowed to lead an away team. Why would he be allowed to place himself in jeopardy in a shuttle? The shuttle is disabled and Picard beams out proving the danger.

Data's relationship with Jenna ends when she explains that even though he's attentive, he's not involved in the way a person with emotions would be. Data accepts this as he would any observation. When Jenna leaves Data's quarters, he busies himself with Spot, his cat.

EPISODE ONE HUNDRED: "REDEMPTION I"

Written by Ronald D. Moore
Directed by Cliff Bole
Guest Cast: Robert O'Reilly, Tony Todd, Barbara March, Gwynyth Walsh, Ben Slack, Nicholas Kepros, J.D. Cullum, Denise Crosby

Worf accepted Discommendation for the betterment of his people with the understanding that one day he would regain his honor. That day arrives when the Duras sisters challenge Gowron for control of the High Council and a civil war breaks out.

Worf takes a leave of absence from Starfleet to join his brother, Kurn, on the side of Gowron. Worf is determined to wait until Gowron desperately needs their support and then force Gowron to restore his honor.

The Duras sisters, who make their last stand in STAR TREK: GENERATIONS, are introduced in this story. They conspire with the Romulans just as their father did before them. The Romulan commander is revealed to be the spitting image of Tasha Yar, a fact that will not be explained in this episode.

Honor is restored to Worf. The story ends on a cliffhanger with the Klingons about to wage civil war over who will control the high council. The excellent episode is the first two-parter to feature Klingons.

SEASON

FIVE

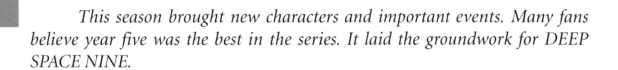

This season brought new characters and important events. Many fans believe year five was the best in the series. It laid the groundwork for DEEP SPACE NINE.

SEASON FIVE

EPISODE ONE HUNDRED ONE: "REDEMPTION II"

Written by Ronald D. Moore
Directed by David Carson
Guest Cast: Denise Crosby, Tony Todd, Barbara March, Gwynth Walsh, J.D. Cullum, Robert O'Reilly, Michael G. Hagerty, Fran Bennett, Nicholas Kepros, Colm Meaney, Timothy Carhart

As the Klingon crisis continues, Worf and Kurn narrowly escape their enemies. Picard argues that the Federation must cut the supply line between the Romulans and the Klingons. The conclusion of "Redemption" keeps the roller coaster story moving with twists and turns right up to the end. It's inevitable that the Federation backed Klingons will win, but it's a well-written story just the same.

Gowron defeats the family Duras when their ties to the Romulans are revealed. It seems that the youth put forth as an illegitimate son of the Duras clan may be phony. The two sisters quickly abandon him after they lose their battle to gain control of the throne.

As expected, Worf returns to the Enterprise at the conclusion of the episode. The fifth season featured no other Klingon episodes.

EPISODE ONE HUNDRED TWO: "DARMOK"

Teleplay by Joe Menosky
Story by Philip Lazebnik and Joe Menosky
Guest Cast: Paul Winfield, Richard Allen, Colm Meaney, Ashley Judd

The Enterprise must negotiate with a difficult race. Previous negotiation attempts failed when the Federation couldn't communicate with the Children of Tama.

Season five begins daring experiments with an unusual story about a race that speaks only in metaphors. I never encountered this idea before. Repeating an element from the original STAR TREK episode "Arena," the captains of the Enterprise and an alien vessel meet face to face on the surface of a planet to settle their differences.

The differences arise from a language barrier in a very unusual and satisfying story. The presentation of communication through metaphors may be difficult for viewers to follow.

EPISODE ONE HUNDRED THREE: "ENSIGN RO"

Teleplay by Michael Piller
Story by Rick Berman & Michael Piller
Directed by Les Landeau
Guest Cast: Michelle Forbes, Scott Marlowe, Frank Collison, Jeffrey Hayenga, Harley Venton, Ken Thorley, Cliff Potts

Admiral Kennelly wants Picard to find Orta, a Bajoran terrorist leader. He wants Orta's attacks stopped. Kennelly assigns Ensign Ro Laren, a Bajoran, to the Enterprise. The former Starfleet officer was court marshaled and sent to prison for an incident on Garon Two.

This episode introduced Michelle Forbes as the controversial Bajoran released from a Federation prison to assist the Enterprise. The story becomes increasingly complex as Ro finds herself manipulated by a Federation admiral. He has a secret deal with the Cardassians. This episode establishes Roas a very interesting character and a welcome addition to the Enterprise.

Michelle Forbes appeared in several more episodes in the fifth season as a semiregular. The producers planned for her to be a regular on DEEP SPACE NINE but never consulted her. She had no interest in a series, and appeared in only one sixth season episode. Her presence is missed. She stole every scene she was in because her character has a hard edge others lack.

Ro Laren is a displaced individual. Her home world, Bajor, was conquered by the Cardassians decades ago. Bajor will become a key element of DEEP SPACE NINE.

Female characters on NEXT GENERATION usually toiled in the shadows of their male counterparts. Ro Laren was created as an individual with both positive and negative traits. She could be abrasive and difficult as well as intelligent and loyal. Her character added energy to the series at the beginning of season five. Many fans feel that season five was the best season because of her presence.

Ensign Ro violated the character stereotype Gene Roddenberry established on NEXT GENERATION. She has the common human foibles that plague 20th Century humanity. She is argumentative and questions orders. She even violates them, although that was played down in subsequent stories. It formed the basis for events when she returned for the crucial seventh season episode "Preemptive Strike."

EPISODE ONE HUNDRED FOUR: "SILICON AVATAR"

Teleplay by Jeri Taylor
Story by Lawrence V. Conley
Directed by Cliff Bole
Guest Cast: Ellen Geer, Susan Dion

The Silicon Avatar first appeared in the otherwise forgettable first season entry "Datalore." It returned in an effective story. Dr. Kila Marr has studied its attacks for years, ever since her young son fell victim in the colony where Data was created.

Dr. Marr devoted her life to catching and destroying it. Scenes between Data and Dr. Kila Marr work well, particularly when Data recalls her son's diary from his memory bank. Dr. Marr blames herself for her son's death. She had allowed him to be raised by friends while she pursued her career.

The episode opens with an effective scene of the Silicon Avatar attacking a world. The Enterprise has dropped off an away team to help colonists. They hide some colonists in a cave, but a woman Riker befriends falls victim.

This story is about an encounter with a strange life form and how a woman deals with her guilt. It is unusual in that while we don't support Dr. Marr's actions, we understand her motivations. In one scene Commander Riker suggests doing what Dr. Marr ultimately does.

EPISODE ONE HUNDRED FIVE: "DISASTER"

Teleplay by Ronald D. Moore
Story by Ron Jarvis & Philip A. Scorza
Directed by Gabrielle Beaumont
Guest Cast: Rosalind Chao, Colm Meaney, Michelle Forbes, Erika Flores, John Christian Graas, Max Supera, Cameron Arnett, Dana Hupp

The Enterprise hits a quantum filament that cuts communications within the ship when emergency procedures go into effect. This is STAR TREK mixed with an Irwin Allen disaster film. Crawling around inside the Enterprise reminds one of THE POSEIDON ADVENTURE.

This true ensemble adventure puts characters cut off from each other into individual dramas. In one the warp core slowly loses stability in the anti-matter chamber, leading to a possible breach. They can't eject the warp core, so Ensign Ro wants to separate the saucer, leaving the rest of the vessel behind. That is exactly what they do in STAR TREK: GENERATIONS.

Early episodes established Picard as a man uncomfortable around children. He is injured and trapped with three frightened preadolescent kids. It's an exercise in teamwork.

Riker and Data try to reach engineering to avert disaster while Worf is trapped in Ten Forward with Keiko O'Brien, who is about to give birth. What would a disaster story be without a pregnant woman?

This ridiculous subplot becomes amusing because Worf learned how to deliver babies from a computer program. He becomes annoyed with Keiko when her body doesn't precisely follow what the programming indicated.

Deanna Troi finally gets a scene of real consequence as the ranking officer on the bridge. Others disagree with her decisions, but she proves right. It offers a moment of growth to Deanna.

EPISODE ONE HUNDRED SIX: "THE GAME"

Teleplay by Brannon Braga
Story by Susan Sackett & Fred Bronson and Brannon Braga
Directed by Corey Allen
Guest Cast: Ashley Judd, Katherine Moffat, Colm Meaney, Patti Yasutake, Wil Wheaton

Riker returns from Risa with an addictive, dangerous video game. When Wesley Crusher determines that the Enterprise has been invaded by the new game, everyone turns against him.

This is a Wesley Crusher episode. He again saves the Enterprise, with a little help. Some fans loved it while others hated it.

The story has similarities to THE INVASION OF THE BODY SNATCHERS movie. The Game takes over everyone on the Enterprise except Wesley. He doesn't like games and avoids playing it while those around him fall under its domination.

Familiar characters suddenly turn bad and gang up on Wesley to force him to play the game. We suspect that this game won't work on Data, and are proven right when Dr. Crusher lures him into her office and shuts him off.

An early scene disturbed some fans. In it Riker enjoys the company of an attractive young woman on Risa. He stares at her as if she is nothing more than pretty meat. While some women were offended, some men knew exactly how Riker felt. She turned out to be the villain of the episode

EPISODE ONE HUNDRED SEVEN: "UNIFICATION I"

Teleplay by Jeri Taylor
Story by Rick Berman & Michael Piller
Directed by Les Landeau
Guest Cast: Joanna Miles, Stephen Root, Graham Jarvis, Malachi Throne, Norman Large, Daniel Roebuck, Erick Avari, Karen Hensel, Mark Lenard, Leonard Nimoy

Year Five brought Mr. Spock to THE NEXT GENERATION in a two-part episode. The script feels rushed as if the story was hastily put into production to air in the November "sweeps month" ratings period. It scored the high ratings they wanted, but the story left a lot to be desired. Spock appears only in the last scene. The writing in part one is better than in part two. The story tells of the death of Sarek, which occurs off-stage.

Mark Lenard performs excellent scenes with Patrick Stewart. One wonders how much better they might have been if they had involved Spock more directly.

The episode supposedly served as a lead-in to STAR TREK VI: THE UNDIS-COVERED COUNTRY released a month later. Since this storyline involves Romulans and the movie deals with Klingons, the only real connection is a remark Spock makes in part two.

"Unification" reveals that Spock left Starfleet to become an ambassador like his father. They are on the outs again.

Part one demonstrates Federation intelligence techniques. Spock is spotted in slightly fuzzy photos from the Romulan homeworld. They fear he has defected.

The original STAR TREK episode "Balance of Terror" first revealed that Romulans and Vulcans are of the same race. It was not followed up on until this episode.

Part one offers a detective story. The Enterprise tracks clues while Data and Picard disguise themselves as Romulans to visit Romulus in a cloaked Klingon ship. The story is much more tightly woven than the conclusion in part two.

EPISODE ONE HUNDRED EIGHT: "UNIFICATION II"

Teleplay by Michael Piller
Story by Rick Berman and Michael Piller
Directed by Cliff Bole
Guest Cast (Additional): Denise Crosby, Vidal Peterson, Harriet Leider

Spock's appearance in the second part is disappointing. After a big build-up, his presence is anticlimactic.

The end of Part 1 promises much, but the resolution fails to deliver. This was too typical of two-part THE NEXT GENERATION episodes. The producers of THE NEXT GENERATION apparently had no idea what to do with Nimoy.

Spock meets with the Romulans. It is an interesting idea. He suggests that the Romulans may be a Vulcan offshoot that left the homeworld centuries ago to establish a separate society. Vulcans overcame a warlike past with a new way of living. The Romulans never abandoned their martial roots. Perhaps they followed the course Vulcans would have if they had not adopted peace and logic as unifying goals.

Secret meetings between Spock and Romulans indicate that some Romulans have a deep interest in their ancestry from ancient Vulcan. The story fails to address whether these Romulans want to adopt Vulcan's pacific ideals and reject Romulan society.

Romulus and Vulcan reuniting peaceably seems to be an impossible dream. Perhaps it is as impossible as Klingons joining the Federation.

The Romulans remain a strict, militaristic society, although they are not of one mind. The Romulan commander, played by Mark Lenard, questioned the wisdom of military dictatorship as early as "Balance of Terror." His first officer fully supported Romulan conquest.

"Unification" exploits this dissension further. The political difficulties of two very different societies forming an alliance becomes submerged in a typical story of betrayal and failure, topped with a few starship explosions.

Spock finally disappears into a cave with his Romulan supporters. He is a figure of legend, an independent operator acting as an ambassador outside the province of the Federation. The Federation has no open dialogue with Romulus. Neither side trusts the other in their armed truce. It is not clear if Vulcan is ready to extend open arms to descendants whose every action reminds them of their brutal past. This remains unexplored.

EPISODE ONE HUNDRED NINE: "A MATTER OF TIME"

Written by Rick Berman
Directed by Paul Lynch
Guest Cast: Matt Frewer, Stefan Gierasch, Sheila Franklin, Ghay Garner

The Enterprise encounters a time traveler who claims to come from the future. He has come to see the events of that particular day but refuses to reveal their nature. Matt Frewer plays the time traveler, Berlinghoff Rasmussen. The fine comic actor starred in the series DOCTOR, DOCTOR and played roles in films including HONEY, I SHRUNK THE KIDS. The character is unusual, different from anyone on NEXT GENERATION.

Clever misdirection keeps you guessing until the truth is revealed in the climax. Frewer's character, an unscrupulous scientist, takes advantage of every opportunity.

The main plot and subplot seem inter-related, but they're not. When the Enterprise brings Dr. Rasmussen's time machine aboard, he refuses to get involved. Picard makes a decision that effects the lives of everyone on the planet Pentara Four.

This is a very different time travel story. It would play well even without the STAR TREK connection.

EPISODE ONE HUNDRED TEN: "NEW GROUND"

Teleplay by Grant Rosenberg
Story by Sara Charno & Stuart Charno
Directed by Robert Scheerer
Guest Cast: Brian Bonsall

The Enterprise arrives at Lemma Two. Doctor Ja'Dar briefs them on the Soliton Wave discovery. The wave will be generated on the planet's surface to propel an unmanned test ship waiting in its path. When the experiment goes wrong and threatens the colony on Lemma Two, the Enterprise races to neutralize the danger. That's the main story.

This is a Worf episode, but not a Klingon episode. Too much of the story focuses on the conflict between Worf and his young son. Rather than solve their problem in a realistic and intelligent manner, Worf saves his son's life. How often are families put into a situation where that conveniently happens to solve a personal problem? It has nothing to do with their underlying problems and solves nothing. Subsequent episodes show them arguing again.

Alexander domesticated Worf. Worf is seen as a father instead of a warrior. It weakened the character. It began with this episode, but future episodes will show Worf as no different from Terrestrial fathers, and duller than most. This episode almost marked the death knell for this character. No new effective Klingon episodes appeared until the end of season six when the old Worf began to re-emerge.

EPISODE ONE HUNDRED ELEVEN: "HERO WORSHIP"

Teleplay by Joe Menosky
Story by Hilary J. Bader
Directed by Patrick Stewart
Guest Cast: Joshua Harris, Harley Venton

The series explored Data in many ways, often contrasting him with humans. Data demonstrates a clear understanding of the human psyche in "Hero Worship." He guides a young boy through trauma when he loses his parents in an accident. The child first blames himself. To escape guilt and pain, he begins to imitate Data. He thinks androids feel no pain.

The sensitive, intelligent teleplay is one of the strongest episodes of year five, a season with many strong episodes.

Deanna Troi tells Data what the boy is going through, and that the boy trusts the android. Data will have to help him face his problems. At first they don't know why the boy imitates Data. They think it is because Data rescued him from beneath wreckage on the Vico.

A moving scene shows Tim telling Data what he thinks happened aboard the Vico. Picard points out that falling against a computer console couldn't have caused damage to the ship. The computers have safeguards to prevent accidental triggering of controls.

Data and Tim save the Enterprise. Many episodes focus on children. They usually present them as interesting people.

EPISODE ONE HUNDRED TWELVE: "VIOLATIONS"

Teleplay by Pamela Gray and Jeri Taylor
Story by Shari Goodhartz & T. Michael and Pamela Gray
Directed by Robert Wiemer
Guest Cast: David Sage, Eve Brenner, Rosalind Chao, Ben Lemon, Rick Fitts, Doug Wert, Craig Benton

A delegation of Ullians, telepathic humanoids, travels aboard the Enterprise. Crew members begin to fall into deathlike comas.

This odd episode presents a rogue telepath who likes to invade the minds of non-telepaths. The mystery becomes repetitious as one regular after another succumbs after experiencing a strange hallucination. The telepath is motivated by resentment of his famous father, but the reason for the competition is not addressed. There are far more interesting stories with telepaths than this one.

EPISODE ONE HUNDRED THIRTEEN: "MASTERPIECE SOCIETY"

Teleplay by Adam Belanoff and Michael Piller
Story by James Kahn and Adam Belanoff
Directed by Rick Kolbe
Guest Cast: Ron Canada, Dey Young, John Synder, Sheila Franklin

A previously unknown colony is a secluded, too-perfect society. A stellar core fragment heads towards their world, Moab IV.

The Enterprise learns that every individual plays a vital role in this utopia. The society cannot deal with the loss of key people, but some want to visit the outside world to experience the changes of the past century.

The leaders oppose disrupting their society. Each person's future is decided before they are born. It seems odd that such a carefully regulated machine wouldn't plan for the loss of human cogs. The problem appears artificial.

The Enterprise must help prepare the colony for the effects of the approaching stellar core fragment, and try to divert the fragment from its course.

This two hundred year old colony must have an interesting history, but we're never let in on it. How could a Federation colony be so isolated? Colonists are surprised by matter transmission. This means "beaming" must be less than two centuries old.

The interesting episode leaves questions unanswered.

EPISODE ONE HUNDRED FOURTEEN: "CONUNDRUM"

Teleplay by Barry Schkolnick
Story by Paul Schiffer
Directed by Les Landau
Guest Cast: Erich Anderson, Michelle Forbes, Liz Vassey, Erick Weiss

The Enterprise investigates subspace signals. Then a small vessel scans the Enterprise. Computers go down as a wave of light sweeps through the inside of the ship. After it passes, everyone suffers from amnesia. The computers tell them they are at war.

This excellent mystery selectively deletes memories from the Enterprise crew and convinces them they are at war with the Lysians. One amusing sequence shows Worf deciding he must be the captain since he's the only Klingon aboard the Enterprise.

The viewer knows something is wrong, but we don't know the reason. Using Lysians makes things more confusing than if it was Klingons or Romulans. Lysians are not as technologically advanced as Starfleet. This gives Picard a clue when he realizes such a foe could not wage war against the Federation.

Characters become reacquainted within the mystery. Riker and Ro Laren normally barely tolerate each other. Now they have an affair. When they regain their memories, Riker is embarrassed and everyone else is amused. Since Riker has been portrayed as a bit of a tom cat, targeting an attractive female is not out of character.

This is an unusual episode with a unique idea. It stands out as one of the best in the fifth season.

EPISODE ONE HUNDRED FIFTEEN: "POWER PLAY"

Teleplay by Rene Balcer and Herbert J. Wright & Brannon Braga
Story by Paul Ruben and Maurice Hurley
Directed by David Livingston
Guest Cast: Rosalind Chal, Colm Meaney, Michelle Forbes, Ryan Reid

Hostile alien entities take over Troi, Data and O'Brien after they beam down to answer a distress signal. Troi claims to be Bryce Shumar of the starship Essex. She wants to get her crew's remains from the planet where their consciousness lie trapped for two hundred years.

The possessed Data, O'Brien and Troi ruthlessly try to take over the Enterprise. They so brutally force their demands that one wonders how they could be former starship officers. The character choices are interesting. Data expresses emotion, but the normally friendly Counselor Troi appears threatening and dangerous.

Bravura performances fill this episode. Regulars got the opportunity to play very different characters. Data seems the most dangerous of the trio, but the story reverses O'Brien's normal personality. He even threatens his wife and child since the inhabiting entity feels nothing towards them.

The captivating episode ends too conveniently, but the story remains powerful in later viewing.

EPISODE ONE HUNDRED SIXTEEN: "ETHICS"

Teleplay by Ronald D. Moore
Story by Sara Charno & Stuart Charno
Directed by Chip Chalmers
Guest Cast: Caroline Kava, Brian Bonsall, Patti Yasutake

Questions arise when Worf's spine is crushed. Dr. Crusher wants to use existing technology to restore most of his motor functions. Dr. Toby Russell, a neuro-geneticist, prefers an experimental new technique, cloning a new spine and transplanting it, a previously untested procedure.

Worf and Alexander face their most important fifth season conflicts in this episode, even though we know he'll be cured by the end of the hour. That's the problem with putting series regulars in jeopardy. The result is inevitable. Had Alexander been crippled, there would have been more room for doubt. The season premiere, "Redemption, Part 2," remains the only true Klingon episode in season five.

"Ethics" qualifies somewhat as a Klingon episode. Klingon culture plays a part in the story when Worf insists on committing suicide. Life as a cripple is dishonorable for Klingons; a warrior prefers death. This must have antagonized handicapped viewers of THE NEXT GENERATION. We've often been told that being "physically challenged" is just another way to be, no less deserving of respect than being completely strong and healthy.

When healthy people are suddenly crippled, they often pass through a brief state of mind when they consider death preferable to life as a cripple. This is particularly true of very active and athletic people. It is a common procedure to have a knockout drug ready and waiting when a newly crippled patient awakens after surgery.

Worf is a warrior from a warrior culture. Being crippled is unthinkable for him. His attitude must be viewed from this perspective. On STAR TREK, alien cultural differences are rarely portrayed in a sympathetic light, or on an equal level with human society.

EPISODE ONE HUNDRED SEVENTEEN: "THE OUTCAST"

Written by Jeri Taylor
Directed by Robert Scheerer
Guest Cast: Melinda Culea, Callan White, Megan Cole

The J'Naii, an androgynous race, contact the Enterprise. They need help finding a missing shuttle. Riker falls in love with a J'Naii, then discovers that gender preferences are illegal in this genderless society.

Soren relates a painful childhood experience. One of her classmates was discovered to prefer males. He was ridiculed, tormented and beaten until the authorities took the boy away. Upon his return, the J'Naii stood before a school assembly and explained how much better he felt after being cured. This terrified Soren. She knew she had to keep her gender orientation secret. "I have had to live a life of pretense and lies," she tells Riker.

This episode took a timid approach. The analogy, and near parable, allowed the producers to have it both ways. It plays as a gay themed story, but it isn't. Most younger fans wouldn't pick up on the real story. Gay teens would. The big speech scene is important because it presents a defense for the predisposition with which a person is born. It articulates the feelings a gay teen struggles with.

Often gay themed stories are censored in the name of "family values." This recently happened to the newspaper strip "For Better Or For Worse" when a fifteen year old boy confessed he is gay and it affected the people around him. A few newspapers declined to run the strip arguing that they are "family" newspapers even though this is a vital issue for families.

Some fans disliked the ending. Riker never mentions the similarity to life on Earth in the 20th Century, even though it made sense for him to come to that conclusion. In dramatic terms, such a statement would have seemed to beat the viewer over the head with the theme. It would have made everything too obvious.

A story such as this is always a tightrope walk. It is better to err on the side of understatement instead of preaching to the converted.

Another criticism is that the androgynous J'Naii were all played by actresses rather than actors. Imagine how much more unnerving the show would have been had androgynous looking males with slight builds portrayed the J'Naii. This, too, would have made the story too tough to take for many fans, particularly since Riker has been shown to be quite a womanizer.

This is the bravest story the series told in twenty-six years of STAR TREK. One flaw in having only actresses portray the J'Naii is that the condemnation of involvement with Riker appears to come from a race of man-hating Lesbians. The episode tries hard, but creates new pitfalls by being too careful.

EPISODE ONE HUNDRED EIGHTEEN: "CAUSE AND EFFECT"

Written by Brannon Braga
Directed by Jonathan Frakes
Guest Cast: Michelle Forbes, Patti Yasutake, Kelsey Grammer

Time travel gets a new STAR TREK twist. The Enterprise is caught in a time loop that recycles each time the starship is destroyed. Director Jonathan Frakes turned a potentially boring repetition into a fascinating episode. He clearly has a firm grasp on the series.

The episode begins with a time loop and the destruction of the Enterprise then breaks for a commercial. After the commercial, it picks up at the beginning again. It works because events repeat with differences and coincidences the crew begin to notice despite having no conscious memory of previous loops. The experimental episode fascinated me.

The weekly poker game plays a key role in this story. Players know what card the other is going to draw. Finally, the cards arrange themselves in a peculiar manner.

The time loop raises a point STAR TREK has dealt with before: the future can be changed. The two TV series set precedent for when time is altered in STAR TREK: GENERATIONS. The original STAR TREK episode "City On The Edge of Forever" showed that the past could be changed. Time travel is pretty tricky, as best illustrated in "Yesterday's Enterprise."

Kelsey Grammer plays the commander of the 23rd Century starship they encounter. He played Fraiser Crane on the hit series CHEERS, and continued the role in his own series. Many STAR TREK fans work in television.

EPISODE ONE HUNDRED NINETEEN: "THE FIRST DUTY"
Written by Ronald D. Moore & Naren Shankar
Directed by Paul Lynch
Guest Cast: Ray Walston, Robert Duncan McNeill, Ed Lauter, Richard Fancy, Jacqueline Brookes, Wil Wheaton

Hotshot Wesley nears graduation at Starfleet Academy. His pristine image crumbles when he helps cover up the death of a friend who dies in an accident. The episode focuses on Wesley and Captain Picard.

Picard returns to Starfleet Academy to visit Wesley after the accident. He meets the old grounds keeper, Boothby, played by Ray Walston. Their discussions reveal much about Picard as a young cadet. They refer to a scandal involving Jean-Luc, which he slipped through. The nature of the scandal is never revealed. It probably didn't involve a reckless maneuver ending in someone's death.

Wesley reluctantly participates in the cover-up. Although he agonizes over his decision, his friends talk him into maintaining the solidarity of the group. He finally confesses under duress. He wouldn't have without pressure from Captain Picard. If Picard hadn't discovered the cover-up, Wesley would've maintained silence. The dead youth would've been regarded as the cause of the accident rather than its victim.

Wesley will never be seen as pristine again. It is an important turning point in his life.

A character from this episode returned in the seventh season episode "Lower Decks." Capt. Picard refuses to let her live down this incident and seems much harsher on her than on Wesley.

EPISODE ONE HUNDRED TWENTY: "COST OF LIVING"
Written by Peter Allan Fields
Directed by Winrich Kolbe
Guest Cast: Majel Barrett, Brian Bonsall, Tony Jay, Carel Struycken, David Oliver, Albie Selznick, Patrick Cronin, Tracy D'Arcy, George Ede, Christopher Halsted

Worf and Alexander continue to argue. Lwaxana tells Troi that she's getting married again and wants the ceremony performed in Ten Forward.

This unfortunate throwback returns to the old style Lwaxana Troi episodes such as "Haven." That episode even included plans for a wedding ceremony. "Haven" mentioned that a Betazoid wedding is performed in the nude, but they didn't follow through. This time they do. Lwaxana arrives at her wedding naked, although she has a different reason for doing this.

The domestication of Worf continues. He and Alexander bicker and complain while Lwaxana tries to smooth things out. Worf even winds up in the holodeck in a mud bath. He doesn't like it.

EPISODE ONE HUNDRED TWENTY-ONE: "THE PERFECT MATE"

Teleplay by Gary Perconte and Michael Piller
Story by Rene Echevarria and Gary Perconte
Directed by Cliff Bole
Guest Cast: Famke Janssen, Tim O'Connor, Max Grodenchik, Mickey Cottrell
Michael Snyder, David Paul Needles, Roger Rignack, Charles Gunning, April Grace

This odd episode tells the story of an empathic metamorph, a woman destined to be a perfect mate for a designated husband. She is also meant to be a perfect sex partner. The plotline recalls the original STAR TREK episode "Elaine of Troyius" as she falls in love with the Captain. Both know she has her duty to perform.

The episode disturbed many female fans. They claim it sanctioned a form of slavery. Actually it was the way this culture worked. Picard says that the Prime Directive prevents them from interfering. This is clearly not an endorsement of the practice by the show but rather a portrayal of a different, but interesting, culture.

Two bumbling Ferengi board the Enterprise in a bungled attempt to steal the metamorph. Max Grodenchik played one of the Ferengi. He later played Quark's brother on DEEP SPACE NINE.

The episode tries very hard but never really works.

EPISODE ONE HUNDRED TWENTY-TWO: "IMAGINARY FRIEND"

Teleplay by Edithe Swensen and Brannon Braga
Story by Jean Louise Matthias & Ronald Wilkerson and Richard Fligel
Directed by Gabrielle Beaumont
Guest Cast: Noley Thornton, Shay Astar, Jeff Allin, Brian Bonsall, Patti Yasutake, Sheila Franklin

Troi talks to Clara Sutter. The little girl tells her about Isabella, her imaginary friend. When the Enterprise enters a strange nebula, Isabella comes to life, and proves potentially dangerous.

Another alien entity slips aboard the Enterprise and causes problems. The entity takes the form of Sara's imaginary friend. No one realizes Isabella has become real until it's almost too late.

NEXT GENERATION episodes about children usually feature adolescent boys, but this one centers on a young girl. It honestly portrays her with dignity.

EPISODE ONE HUNDRED TWENTY-THREE: "I, BORG"

Written by Rene Echevarria
Directed by Robert Lederman
Guest Cast: Jonathan Del Arco

The Borg get a human face. Borg begin life as human, then are altered to be part of the cybernetic group mind. The Enterprise treats an injured Borg found on a wrecked scout ship.

Captain Picard never makes a Captain's Log report to Starfleet Command apprising them of the situation. Perhaps, recalling his abduction, he tried to cover up decisions he might make in anger towards the Borg.

Geordi talks to the Borg youth, and even names him "Hugh." "Hugh" learns individuality from Geordi.

When Hugh turns to Geordi at the end, he seems to have retained his individuality, even after being assimilated into the collective. Free will could prove destructive to the Borg.

Perhaps the Borg will be infected with the idea of individual beings by Hugh. He might be the seed for a new type of Borg. "I, Borg" leaves many possibilities for future stories. It enriched the creative tapestry of the series.

This episode formed the background for events that began to unfold in the season six cliffhanger, "Descent." Hugh the Borg reappeared at the beginning of season seven.

EPISODE ONE HUNDRED TWENTY-FOUR: "THE NEXT PHASE"

Written by Ronald D. Moore
Directed by David Carson
Guest Cast: Michelle Forbes, Thomas Kopache, Susanna Thompson, Shelby Leverington, Brian Cousins, Kenneth Meseroll

Geordi and Ro are declared dead after an apparent transporter accident. They are actually invisible and intangible. This Romulan episode sends the Enterprise to lend assistance to Romulans on a disabled ship. The Romulans decide they must dispose of the Enterprise.

This episode works unless you ask too many questions. How can Ro and Geordi see anything if they're invisible and intangible? Light would not reflect off of their optic nerve. How do they speak to each other in voices only they can hear and how do they hear what anyone else says? If they can move through bulkheads, why don't they fall through the hull of the Enterprise and out into space? How long could they survive in a non-corporeal state? Pseudo-science stretches to the breaking point in this one.

This excellent action story forces Geordi and Ro Laren to undo what's happened to them to warn the Enterprise crew of danger. It's also a good character episode. The two become friends once Geordi convinces Ensign Ro that they're not dead. For a time

Ro Laren believes this is what death is like. She was ready to accept her state as The Next Phase of existence.

EPISODE ONE HUNDRED TWENTY-FIVE: "THE INNER LIGHT"

Teleplay by Morgan Gendel and Peter Allan Fields
Story by Morgan Gendel
Directed by Peter Lauritson
Guest Cast: Margot Rose, Richard Riehle, Scott Jaeck, Jennifer Nash, Patti Yasutake, Daniel Stewart

Fans still discuss this experimental episode. An alien space probe zaps Captain Picard. He is apparently drawn a thousand years into the past to live the remainder of his life as a husband and father. Then he reawakens on the Enterprise and finds that he's been unconscious for 20 minutes!

The mystery keeps fans arguing over what happened during the climax of the story. Picard, still on the alien world, sees people who died during his years there. The unusual story took many worthwhile intellectual risks.

Looking back now, it seems that the memories of the man named Kamen were projected into Picard's mind while he lay unconscious. He believed he was Kamen. It was that dying race's way of leaving a legacy for other worlds.

An interesting touch is that Kamen knew how to play the flute, and, after this incident, Jean-Luc can play the flute. He couldn't before.

The strangest STAR TREK story ever forces you to think. It's worth the effort.

EPISODE ONE HUNDRED TWENTY-SIX: "TIME'S ARROW"
Part One

Teleplay by Joe Menosky and Michael Piller
Story by Joe Menosky
Directed by Les Landau
Guest Cast: Jerry Hardin, Michael Aron, Barry Kivel, Ken Thorley, Sheldon Peters Wolfchild, Jack Murdock, Marc Alaimo, Milt Tarver, Michael Hungerford

Excavations beneath San Francisco reveal evidence of alien visitors on Earth in the late 19th Century— along with Data's severed head!

"Time's Arrow" hooks you with a story about Data's death. This complicated tale involves 19th Century San Francisco, Mark Twain, Guinan and strange aliens. Fans often call the episode "Data's Head," a play on the original STAR TREK episode "Spock's Brain."

It was an interesting episode that ended in a cornucopia of eerie effects. Picard and his team follow Data to Nineteenth Century San Francisco. The android meets a slightly younger Guinan and the obligatory Mark Twain. The show missed the boat with this obvious choice. San Francisco's benevolent madman of the period, the Emperor Norton, would have made an interesting character. The bizarre situations, and striking imagery, promised an exciting conclusion.

SEASON

SIX

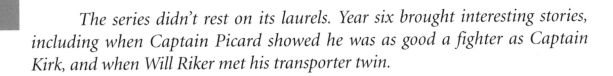

The series didn't rest on its laurels. Year six brought interesting stories, including when Captain Picard showed he was as good a fighter as Captain Kirk, and when Will Riker met his transporter twin.

SEASON SIX

EPISODE ONE HUNDRED TWENTY-SEVEN: "TIME'S ARROW" PART 2

Written by Jeri Taylor
From a story by Joe Menosky
Directed by Les Landeau
Guest Cast: Jerry Hardin, Michael Aron, Barry Kivel, Ken Thorley, Sheldon Peters Wolfchild, Jack Murdock, Marc Alaimo, Milt Tarver, Michael Hungerford

Samuel Clemens wants to expose aliens in 19th Century San Francisco. The aliens are Data and Guinan. Meanwhile, Capt. Picard, Lt. Riker, Dr. Crusher and Geordi arrive after passing through the Devidian time portal.

The meandering story in part two completely undercut the excitement in the first part as it lurched from one scene to another. It dragged Samuel Clemens along for an unnecessary ride. The build-up turned into a letdown as the alien life-force thieves never get a personality.

All the loose ends are tied up in a perfunctory manner without clever twists and turns. Samuel Clemens could be cut from the script and the story would remain exactly the same. While characters acknowledge Twain's presence, he doesn't effect the plot!

The sixth season of THE NEXT GENERATION opened with a dismally pointless conclusion to "Time's Arrow." The writers seemed incapable of successfully completing the intriguing mysteries in the first half. The plot quickly fizzles out, giving the cast little to do other than wear period costumes.

EPISODE ONE-HUNDRED TWENTY-EIGHT: "REALM OF FEAR"

Written by Brannon Braga
Directed by Cliff Bole
Guest Cast: Dwight Schultz

The Enterprise goes to the Igo sector to search for the lost U.S.S. Yosemite. This episode features the return of Reginald Barclay, the crewman first seen in "Hollow Pursuits." Barclay still has problems, including a phobia about the transporter. When he reports seeing something while inside the transporter beam, he meets skepticism. His accurate observations create a surprising twist ending.

This mystery concerns the fate of the Yosemite's crew and what is living in the transporter beam. The two are related.

O'Brien talks to Barclay in an amusing concluding scene. They discuss phobias and he mentions that he used to be afraid of spiders. Then he shows Barclay his pet spider, Reginald. It turns out Barclay is also afraid of spiders.

This is a much better than "Time's Arrow, part 2."

EPISODE ONE-HUNDRED TWENTY-NINE: "MAN OF THE PEOPLE"

Written by Frank Abatemarco
Directed by Winrich Kolbe
Guest Cast: Chip Lucia, Stephanie Erb

The Enterprise responds to a ship in distress, under attack near the planet Rekag-Seronia. Rekag-Seronia is divided by growing political conflicts that threaten Federation trade routes. One passenger, Ves Alkar, is a Lumerian ambassador going to end the conflict. The ambassador carries a deadly secret.

This odd episode unsuccessfully features Deanna Troi. She's linked to Ves Alkar in a bizarre way. It leads to strange scenes of her slowly going insane as Alkar leaches emotions from others to maintain his own sanity. This is turned against him at the end.

EPISODE ONE HUNDRED THIRTY: "RELICS"

Written by Ronald D. Moore
Directed by Alexander Singer
Guest Cast: James Doohan

The Enterprise enters an abandoned Dyson sphere. Matters get complicated when they try to leave.

The other relic is Scotty. Gregarious as ever, he tries to fit in, but soon finds there's not much for him on this new Enterprise. There's fine comedic interplay between James Doohan and LeVar Burton as Scotty repeatedly tries to help but only gets in the way. Geordi doesn't want to offend anyone, but he's hard pressed. Scotty finally understands and becomes despondent.

The Enterprise can't escape the Dyson sphere. Geordi needs Scotty's help. Scotty tells Geordi to stop giving Captain Picard accurate estimates of how long a job will take. Scotty always multiplies his estimates to make himself look like a miracle worker!

Everything works out. Scotty feels needed, and soon he's on his way again, after a seventy-five-year delay. Retirement is out of the question; there's too much to learn in this new age.

James Doohan portrays Scotty as charming and humorous. The character gets better scenes than in recent STAR TREK movies. He doesn't bang his head on a bulkhead, and he's never even been on this Enterprise before!

"Relics" portrayed Scotty better than any episode of the original series. He gets a warm send-off from the crew of the Enterprise-D, including a kiss from Deanna. This seems odd since he never shared a scene with Deanna, but the original script included such a scene. In that trimmed scene, Deanna visits Scotty and asks if he wants to know what happened to his friends and family during the past seventy-five years. Scotty doesn't want to know, claiming he isn't ready.

Deleting that scene detracts from "Relics." It would have addressed the issue. Without it, it seems strange that no mention is made of the fates of his friends. Spock's activities are probably classified, but Scotty's lack of curiosity is odd.

Scotty's crossover in "Relics" is better written than that of Spock in "Unification." James Doohan gets a chance to act for a change, particularly in portraying the character as a man out of time; an old man who doesn't fit into this new world.

He finally finds a way, opening future possibilities. Fans still talk about the scene in the holodeck when Scotty resurrects the bridge of the original starship Enterprise. It is an amazing thing to see again. The author added elements to the holodeck scene in the novelization of "Relics," including Scotty talking to Kirk and Spock.

EPISODE ONE-HUNDRED THIRTY-ONE: "SCHISMS"

Written by Brannon Braga
From a story by Ronald Wilkerson & Jean Matthias
Directed by Robert Wiemer

The Enterprise arrives at the globular cluster known as the Amargosa Diaspora. Crewmen experience strange problems, including disappearances while asleep.

This is one of the most unusual episodes in the seven years of NEXT GENERATION. Riker suffers from strange dreams and is always tired. It is disturbing when Dr. Crusher announces that Riker's arm has been secretly surgically removed and reattached.

Crew members only subconsciously remember what is done to them. They later have violent reactions to commonplace objects that trigger submerged memories. This leads to a clever use of the holodeck. It recreates pieces of memory until it reconstructs an alien operating theater. It deepens the mystery.

The secret is a strange one. Riker and other crewmen have disappeared into a dimensional pocket with alien experimenters. The episode never reveals the nature of the aliens. Something escapes after the dimensional pocket is closed. It is never explained. The story seems to originate from current reports of alien abduction.

EPISODE ONE HUNDRED THIRTY-TWO: "TRUE Q"

Written by Rene Echevarria
Directed by Robert Scherrer
Guest Cast: Olivia D'Abo, John de Lancie

A new crew member, 18 year old Amanda Rogers, joins the Enterprise while the vessel flies to the Argolis Cluster. Amanda's parents supposedly died when she was an infant. Actually Q had taken human form to live on Earth. The scene when Amanda reveals her powers in front of everyone to save the ship is dramatic. Q manufactured the event to force her out into the open.

Q appears as an agent of his Continuum, sent to test Amanda and present her with an ultimatum: join the Q and embrace your powers, or live as a human and renounce them utterly. The only other alternative is death. Since Amanda's parents, "retired" Q living on Earth, were killed by the forces of the Continuum, it would seem that Q can be killed, although, perhaps, only by another Q. Amanda chooses humanity. Q tests her until she succumbs to the temptation and uses her power. Then she must admit that she is a Q. "True Q" delivered a new twist on the old reprobate.

The scenes when Amanda experiments with her power, including using it to make Riker love her, demonstrate the dichotomy she suffers between being human and Q. She has feelings and a sense of conscience notably absent from Q.

A dark subplot emerges. Q remains to decide whether Amanda will be allowed to live. He points out that the Continuum takes responsibility for its members. A Q-human half-breed is new to their experience. This subplot was almost excised from the script.

EPISODE ONE HUNDRED THIRTY-THREE: "RASCALS"

Teleplay by Allison Hock
From a story by Ward Botsford, Diana Dru Botsford & Michael Piller
Directed by Adam Nimoy
Guest Cast: David Tristan Birkin, Brian Bonsall, Michael Snyder

The transporter turns Picard, Ensign Ro, Guinan and Keiko O'Brien into children. They outsmart Ferengi trying to steal the Enterprise.

The Ferengi have enough weaponry and knowledge to capture the Enterprise. They plan to sell it to the Romulans but are defeated by the four pint-sized crewmen, Alexander and other shipboard children. Riker and the others look ineffectual. It was supposed to be amusing.

It marked the last appearance of Ensign Ro until her appearance in season seven's "Preemptive Strike." The writers even discussed keeping Ensign Ro as a child on the series. Fortunately, clearer heads prevailed.

David Tristan Birkin plays Jean-Luc. He previously played Rene Picard in the season four episode "Family."

EPISODE ONE HUNDRED THIRTY-FOUR: "A FISTFUL OF DATAS"

Written by Robert Hewitt Wolfe and Brannon Braga
From a story by Robert Hewitt Wolfe.
Directed by Patrick Stewart
Guest Cast: Brian Bonsall

This episode must have been much more fun to make than watch. A programming glitch causes Data to infect the holodeck. Worf and Alexander are trapped in a

Western with characters that all look like Data, even the women. They must play out the cliché to its conclusion before the holodeck will shut down. Worf, the domesticated Klingon, is a painful sight.

Alexander got more cloying as time went on. The boy never acted like a Klingon, and Worf also began acting less Klingon. Subsequent episodes attempted to remedy this.

EPISODE ONE HUNDRED THIRTY-FIVE: "THE QUALITY OF LIFE"
Written by Naren Shankar
Directed by Jonathan Frakes
Guest Cast: Ellen Bry

The Enterprise visits a space station to monitor a massive project, the Tyan particle fountain. They find small robots called exocomps. Data decides that they are self-aware and refuses to allow them to come to harm.

In this strange episode, Data insists that a new type of droid is alive. The self-aware robots refuse to risk their "lives." The story fails to convince the viewer, particularly since Data was not concerned when holodeck characters wanted to live.

The episode contains a contradiction. Data won't endanger the exocomps to save Picard and Riker. His programming includes the Three Laws of Robotics, one of which says that a robot cannot allow a human to come to harm by either direct action or inaction. Data violated that directive in this episode.

EPISODE ONE-HUNDRED THIRTY-SIX: "CHAIN OF COMMAND"
Part One
Written by Ronald D. Moore
From a story by Frank Abatemarco
Directed by Robert Scheerer
Guest Cast: Ronny Cox, David Warner

Vice-Admiral Nechayev wants Picard to resign and undertake a secret mission. The Federation believes Cardassians will invade a disputed system, but don't know which one. Dr. Crusher and Worf accompany Picard, but no one else aboard the Enterprise will know the purpose of their absence.

Picard is replaced by Captain Jellico, played by Ronny Cox. This highly skilled captain lacks interpersonal skills. He doesn't care whether he is liked, but does one good thing. He makes Troi stop wearing her ugly outfit and put on a uniform like everyone else. Troi keeps the uniform for the duration of the series.

The reason for dragging a Starfleet captain into such an undertaking seems contrived. Picard is an expert in metagenic weapons — and no one else is? If Picard wasn't sent on the mission, he couldn't be captured by David Warner, who plays the Cardassian Gul Madred.

David Warner has often played villains, particularly in such films as TIME AFTER TIME, TRON and TIME BANDITS. One of his rare protagonists appeared in the late '70s film THE OMEN. He wasn't seen much on screen in the mid-1980s, but then suddenly became almost a STAR TREK regular, playing different supporting roles in STAR TREK V: THE FINAL FRONTIER and STAR TREK VI: THE UNDISCOVERED COUNTRY, and this major role as Gul Madred. The Cardassian inquisitor proved particularly memorable.

Ronny Cox played Captain Jellico. He hasn't appeared often in films or television in recent years. He gained recognition in the 1970s in a variety of roles, including a supporting role in the movie DELIVERANCE.

EPISODE ONE HUNDRED THIRTY-SEVEN: "CHAIN OF COMMAND" Part Two

Written by Frank Abatemarco
Directed by Les Landeau
Guest Cast: David Warner, Ronny Cox

The Cardassians drug and torture Picard to get information on his mission. They already know all about it as they tricked the Federation into sending him. The torture sequences allow Patrick Stewart to deliver fine performances. His work in THE NEXT GENERATION for this season should have been nominated for an Emmy.

This episode also demonstrates that humanity in the 24th Century is not perfect. Ronny Cox, as the new Captain of the Enterprise, continually clashes with Riker. The new captain labels Riker unfit to be a First Officer.

This second part focuses on adversaries. Gul Madred subjects Jean-Luc to brutal torture. They implant a pain device beneath Picard's skin. Before acting for the episode, Patrick Stewart consulted Amnesty International about the psychological effects of real torture sessions on torturer and victim.

Commander Riker and Captain Jellico become adversaries. Riker talks back to Jellico too many times and is relieved of duty. The most skillful pilot on the Enterprise, Riker, uses a shuttle to lay anti-matter mines. Despite clashes with Riker, Jellico is not a villain. He has a different command style than Picard. It proves equally effective. Jellico deliberately distances himself from his fellow officers and seems more strictly military in breeding.

The torture scenes between Gul Madred and Jean-Luc form the heart of the episode. We've never seen Picard this way before, both helpless and defiant, in pain, yet unbeaten. His discussions with his torturer form the crux of the story, particularly when the Cardassian's daughter enters the room where Picard is imprisoned in front of Gul Madred.

"Chain of Command" brought the Cardassians into the foreground as major participants in the STAR TREK universe.

EPISODE ONE HUNDRED THIRTY-EIGHT: "SHIP IN A BOTTLE"

Written by Rene Echevarria
Directed by Alexander Singer
Guest Cast: Daniel Davis, Dwight Schultz, Stephanie Beacham

In "Elementary Dear Data," Data used the holodeck to create a representation of Sir Arthur Conan Doyle's Prof. Moriarty, the notorious enemy of Sherlock Holmes. By presenting Moriarty twice, STAR TREK used the character more often than his creator Arthur Conan Doyle did! Few realize that Prof. Moriarty appeared in only one Sherlock Holmes story, "The Final Problem." He was so strong a character that he's been used repeatedly in movies and elsewhere ever since.

While Doyle portrayed Moriarty as a black-hearted villain, THE NEXT GENERATION makes him something more than that. Moriarty is a man obsessed with remaining alive. He exhibits love and compassion, but he's willing to go to any length to preserve his existence.

Data argued for recognition as a lifeform for the droids in "The Quality of Life," but refuses Moriarty the same privilege. Moriarty is aware of his own existence and wants to be more than a program on the holodeck.

"Ship In A Bottle" has many interesting twists and turns, particularly the conclusion. The two TNG episodes form a perfect, self-contained whole.

EPISODE ONE HUNDRED THIRTY-NINE: "AQUIEL"

Written by Brannon Braga & Ronald D. Moore
From a story by Jeri Taylor
Directed by Cliff Bole
Guest Cast: Renee Jones

This episode focuses on Geordi. The Enterprise makes a routine stop at a space station near the border with the Klingon empire. The station is deserted. Two officers stationed aboard the station seem to have disappeared. They find a live dog, and a glob of cellular residue that Dr. Crusher reports is the remains of a missing officer.

This episode spotlights Geordi. He falls in love with an African American woman suspected of murder. The story seems patterned after the '40s thriller LAURA. Geordi falls in love with the computer logs left by the missing Lt. Aquiel, only to have her turn up alive halfway through the episode.

An interesting ending fails to make up for slack writing throughout the episode.

EPISODE ONE-HUNDRED FORTY: "FACE OF THE ENEMY"

Written by Naren Shankar
From a story by Rene Eschevarria

Directed by Gabrielle Beaumont
Guest Cast: Carolyn Seymour, Scott MacDonald

This is the first interesting episode featuring Troi. "Power Play" showed the actress at work with more substantial material. "Face Of The Enemy" finally let her fully demonstrate her talent.

In the teaser, Troi awakens to discover she has turned into a Romulan. It prepares us for something unusual. The episode doesn't let us down. It takes us aboard a Romulan ship and shows us life among the Romulans. No episode since "Balance of Terror" offered anything even remotely similar.

The story touches on elements introduced in the fifth season's "Unification." Spock is mentioned, along with members of the Romulan reunification underground.

This episode also shows life aboard a Romulan ship. A member of the Romulan secret police is posted aboard each vessel to keep officers loyal.

EPISODE ONE HUNDRED FORTY-ONE: "TAPESTRY"

Written by Ronald D. Moore
Directed by Les Landeau
Guest Cast: John de Lancie, Ned Vaughn

Jean-Luc Picard suffers a life-threatening injury and lies near death on the operating table as Dr. Crusher and her medical team struggle to revive him. Meanwhile, Picard finds himself in a glowing, white landscape, a classic near-death experience marred by one glaring exception: Q. He benevolently greets Picard with two startling pieces of bad news: "You're dead and I'm God."

Q allows Picard to relive a crucial incident in his youth that led to his artificial heart. Picard again confronts whether he should help his friend Corey rig a gambling game to get back at Nausiccan rowdies. He also faces his unresolved relationship with the woman Marta. Doing the right thing with Corey leads to complications. Sleeping with Marta, which he did not do in real life, adds more bitterness to this early relationship.

His life doesn't proceed well. It was obviously the turning point that led the young, brash Jean-Luc Picard to change his life. It had led to his becoming a thoughtful leader of men.

Q tells Picard that he is God. Q are obviously more highly evolved than humans. STAR TREK never answers the question of their divinity. It seems likely that in a Gene Roddenberry universe, they wouldn't be gods but an evolutionary niche higher than mere mortals.

The ending leaves the story open to interpretation. Was it all a hallucination? Q disappears after Picard awakens. It's a good story, though, and includes a particularly violent scene when the young Picard is stabbed in the back and the blade protrudes from his chest.

EPISODE ONE HUNDRED FORTY-TWO: "Birthright" Part One

Written by Brannon Braga
Directed by Winrich Kolbe
Guest Cast: Siddig El Fadil, James Cromwell

The Federation takes charge of space station Deep Space Nine orbiting Bajor. The Enterprise assists Bajorans on the surface in need of technical assistance following the destructive evacuation of the Cardassians. On the station, Worf meets a man who claims to know that his supposedly long dead father is a prisoner of the Romulans.

This is the first good Klingon episode in two years. It explores the importance of heritage to Worf. The episode was clearly created as a handy crossover with DEEP SPACE NINE. It becomes much more because the space station only appears at the beginning of part one. Dr. Bashir appears in an Enterprise subplot.

Worf is shocked to learn that his father might be a prisoner and not dead. This revelation brings great shame. A Klingon prefers death to captivity. A Klingon's entire family would be disgraced if a warrior believed dead was found alive after years of imprisonment. The importance of this philosophy becomes evident in part two.

Worf refuses to believe his father is alive, but it gnaws at him. He is granted a leave of absence to investigate.

The episode shows a side of the Romulans not displayed in past stories.

EPISODE ONE HUNDRED FORTY-THREE: "BIRTHRIGHT" Part Two

Written by Rene Echevarria
Directed by Dan Curry
Guest Cast: Alan Scarfe, Richard Herd, Christine Rose, Sterling Macer, Jr., Jennifer Gatti

Worf forces information about his father's whereabouts from a captive. It leads to a moon under the control of Romulans, a prison world. Klingon prisoners age as their children grow up unaware of Klingon customs. The Klingons in the Romulan prison camp do not want to be rescued. They know returning to the homeworld would bring disgrace. Worf wants to teach the Klingon children the truth about their heritage.

Romulans are portrayed as benevolent. The commander volunteers to watch over the Klingons and give up his own career. He even takes a Klingon wife and has a half Klingon-half Romulan daughter. This is shocking to Worf. He eventually explains to her that she would not be accepted on other worlds. Klingons and Romulans would view a half-breed as an abomination.

The old Worf returns. He picks up cherished Klingon weapons turned into plowshares and tells the history of each one to the Klingon teenagers. He fires their imaginations, teaching them Klingon pride. In the final confrontation, Klingon youths choose to stand by Worf regardless of the consequences. It validates Worf's beliefs and sense of self.

This interesting story gives Worf a chance to act like a true Klingon for the first time in two years. It made up for seeing Worf dressed in a cowboy hat in "A Fistful of Datas."

EPISODE ONE HUNDRED FORTY-FOUR: "STARSHIP MINE"

Written by Morgan Gendel
Directed by Cliff Bole
Guest Cast: David Spielberg

The Enterprise docks at the Remmler Array. It is scheduled to be cleared of baryon particles. Picard discovers intruders in his cabin. He battles them while the rest of the crew is held hostage on the planet below.

The creative talent decided to show that Captain Kirk wasn't the only two-fisted Enterprise captain. Picard is trapped aboard the Enterprise facing two deadly foes. It is DIE HARD on a starship.

A lethal decontamination ray slowly sweeps the length of the supposedly evacuated starship. Picard uses new and old weapons as ruthlessly as the criminals he fights.

An interesting scene shows Data hearing about a boring diplomat. He deliberately engages the diplomat in pointless conversation to learn how to talk endlessly without saying anything. The funny scene offers excellent verbal humor.

Picard is captured in his civilian clothes and claims that he is Mott, the ship's barber. When he escapes and sets traps for his pursuers, they soon decide he knows too much to be just a barber.

The episode ends with a cliffhanger. Picard is saved with barely a moment to spare. NEXT GENERATION veered away from the all out action stories common on the original STAR TREK. This episode showed that the series could deliver truly exciting change of pace stories.

EPISODE ONE HUNDRED FORTY-FIVE: "LESSONS"

Written by Ronald Wilkerson & Jean Louise Matthias
Directed by Robert Weimer
Guest Cast: Wendy Hughes

While on night watch, Picard meets Lt. Commander Nella Daren, the new chief of the Stellar Sciences department. Picard finds her more interesting at every meeting.

This episode is a character study. It shows what happens when a captain falls in love with a member of his crew. He begins granting her special dispensation, until she insists on being treated like everyone else, including being part of a dangerous mission.

The writers crafted a believable relationship. Scenes are effectively underplayed. In a reference to the episode "Inner Light," we see Jean-Luc playing the flute. At one point Nella has her portable keyboard and Picard his flute. They play a private duet deep in the bowels of the ship. Then, when the music stops. . . .

Her dangerous mission is on a planet ravaged by firestorms. An unusually large storm endangers a scientific outpost. It must be evacuated with the help of the Enterprise. Teams beam down to place deflectors to slow the storm.

This is a very effective story, particularly when Picard believes his love has died on the mission. She beams up at the last minute, one of the few survivors. When she chooses to leave the Enterprise because of the complications in their relationship, it demonstrates the complexities of command. The final scene in most episodes is usually of the Enterprise, but this one ends focused on Picard.

Picard is still alone, with no family or prospect of having one. It forms the crux of a subplot in the 1994 film STAR TREK: GENERATIONS.

EPISODE ONE HUNDRED FORTY-SIX: "THE CHASE"
Written by Joe Menosky
From a story by Ronald Moore & Joe Menosky
Directed by Jonathan Frakes
Guest Cast: Norman Lloyd, Linda Thorson, John Cothran Jr., Maurice Roeves, Salome Jens

Some fans express disappointment with year six. It was at least as good as season five. A few weak episodes appeared alongside many strong, imaginative ones. This mystery adventure has a miraculous outcome.

The story begins simply. Picard's old archeology teacher, Professor Galen, pays a visit to the Enterprise. Galen offers to share his latest discoveries with Jean-Luc if Picard will accompany the professor on his newest exploration. This meeting is both touching and fascinating as Picard examines an ancient artifact. He shows an appreciation of the beauty of this rarity only a true connoisseur could express.

Norman Lloyd is perfect as Picard's old archeology teacher. Thirty years before Picard had been an extraordinary student. Galen never understood Picard's decision to pursue starship command instead of archeology. When Prof. Galen visits the Enterprise he tries to get Picard to leave with him on the mission of a lifetime, but he won't reveal the mission. Picard refuses to accompany him. When Prof. Galen is murdered, Picard chooses to find the killers and solve the mystery. The riddle involves the origin of many races in the Federation, making this a key episode in the entire STAR TREK milieu.

"The Chase" story could easily have filled a two-part adventure. The taught story works perfectly as a single episode thriller without subplots. It is unusual on this series.

While searching for Prof. Galen's discovery, the Enterprise encounters Cardassians and Klingons. Each has their own idea about the nature of the secret. What they believe reveals much about each race.

EPISODE ONE HUNDRED FORTY-SEVEN: "FRAME OF MIND"

Written by Brannon Braga
Directed by Jim Conway
Guest Cast: Andrew Prine, Gary Werntz, David Selburg, Susanna Thompson

Riker is in an insane asylum, patiently trying to convince his doctor that he's better. As Riker becomes increasingly angry, we see that he's on stage in the theatre aboard the Enterprise. Or is he?

This unusual episode keeps us guessing as it plays with reality. It returns to themes touched on in "First Contact." A disguised Riker beams down to an alien world in political upheaval. He is discovered and held captive.

Jonathan Frakes displays strong acting talents as he is first in a play, then he's not, and then he isn't sure. Frakes delivers a convincing performance as manipulations of reality prey on Riker.

Splintering image special effects allow one illusion to shatter and be replaced by another. They are quite unusual. I'd never seen it used before.

This psychological thriller is extremely effective and quite memorable.

EPISODE ONE HUNDRED FORTY-EIGHT: "SUSPICIONS"

Written by Joe Menosky and Naren Shankar
Directed by Cliff Bole
Guest Cast: Peter Slutsker, James Horan, Joan Stuart Morris, Tricia O'Neil

When Guinan visits Dr. Crusher, Beverly is packing to return to Earth. She faces a formal hearing on charges of violating medical ethics, disobeying a direct order and causing an interstellar incident.

The story centers on Dr. Crusher. Secondary elements are more captivating than the primary murder mystery. A Ferengi scientist appears for the first time. He's completely unlike Ferengi businessmen and starship personnel and is not an obnoxious cartoon. The interesting character is killed too quickly. A shuttle in the episode is named the "Justman," a reference to Bob Justman, a producer on the '60s STAR TREK.

A shield is supposed to allow shuttle craft to enter the corona of a star without peril to occupants. The device appears to fail, but more is going on than meets the eye. Only Dr. Crusher believes it.

The episode reveals an aspect of Ferengi culture. They forbid autopsies because the family of the deceased does the cutting and body parts are sold to honor the dead.

Beverly Crusher risks her life to solve this mystery.

EPISODE ONE HUNDRED FORTY-NINE: "RIGHTFUL HEIR"

Written by Ronald D. Moore
From a story by James E. Brooks
Directed by Winrich Kolbe
Guest Cast: Kevin Conway, Robert O'Reilly

Worf stars in his second Klingon story of the sixth season. In "Birthright" Worf encountered Klingons out of touch with their past. He now feels inadequate and wants to get closer to his own heritage. This leads to the world to which Kahless promised to return. Worf witnesses the resurrection.

Kevin Conway portrays the legendary Klingon hero, Kahless. He appears to return to life and claims the Klingon Empire. The third season classic STAR TREK episode "The Savage Curtain" featured the same character, played there by Robert Herron.

"Rightful Heir" revived the same character with a different twist. Perhaps the entity in "The Savage Curtain" recreated Kahless from the human point of view. Here, seen from the perspective of fellow Klingons, Kahless is anything but evil. Kahless is a part of Klingon culture, not a stereotyped villain. To the Klingons he is a hero.

Comparing the Kahless of STAR TREK's "The Savage Curtain" and THE NEXT GENERATION's "Rightful Heir" shows the differences between the two shows. THE NEXT GENERATION examines alien cultures in greater depth. The Klingons are warlike and aggressive but they are also honorable. THE NEXT GENERATION built on the foundation of STAR TREK.

Worf first encounters Kahless when he goes to a Klingon monastery for a religious ritual. Kahless appears in the flesh after millennia. He wants to fix the Klingon Empire. Gowron, the current ruler, is less than thrilled when Worf, once one of his supporters, seems prepared to side with Kahless and the monks. Kahless is a dynamic character, confident enough to endure various tests of his authenticity. Worf is torn between the charisma of this legend-made-flesh and the dictates of logic.

This episode highlights deficiencies in the character of Worf. In "Birthright" Worf encountered peaceful Klingons who rejected their warlike heritage. Worf went to the Klingon monastery to contemplate disturbing issues that incident raised.

Worf is a Klingon serving on a Federation vessel as a symbol of peace and unity. Klingons need to move towards a peaceful future. Yet Worf is determined to hold on to a past he didn't even grow up with. He was raised by humans. Perhaps we're supposed to think Worf overcompensates because some Klingons accuse him of being a lapdog for Starfleet.

EPISODE ONE HUNDRED FIFTY: "SECOND CHANCES"

Written by Rene Echevarria
From a story by Michael A. Medlock
Directed by LeVar Burton
Guest Cast: Mae Jemison

It could have been a cliché. How many times did a duplicate Kirk lead to trouble? When Commander Riker meets his double, it's not an evil twin or an impostor. It's a very intriguing drama.

Riker literally meets himself. . . but a self whose life followed a different course for the past eight years. Eight years ago, a transporter accident created a double. Neither knew of the other until now. They are physically identical.

The story falls short in that both Will Rikers accept their double without turmoil. After the initial shock, they accept their fate. They do get on each other's nerves. This situation would make the average person extremely uncomfortable. Even Worf and Data discuss the bizarre situation. The Klingon admits he would not enjoy meeting his own double.

Deanna Troi might have become a point of contention between them. Instead Commander Will Riker's platonic interest illustrates emotional differences between the two men. Lt. Riker is what Commander Riker might have been had he made different choices in life. One of those choices was Deanna Troi.

Deanna responds favorably to Lt. Riker. This is far more interesting than if she had remained distant and aloof. This episode captures the essence of STAR TREK. It portrays a plausible future in which almost anything is possible, particularly on a human level.

While there is some initial friction between the two Rikers, they are not enemies. The second Riker is not out to take over the Enterprise or to harm his counterpart. He wants to get on with his life. So does the familiar Riker. Drama in "Second Chances" arises without clichés. It counters the usual devices of STAR TREK. "Second Chances" is an excellent tale of the NEXT GENERATION.

Both remain alive at the end, turning the cliché on its head. The delightful episode plays to our expectations and then does the opposite. The second Riker, who calls himself "Thomas," appeared again in the third season DEEP SPACE NINE episode "Defiant."

EPISODE ONE HUNDRED FIFTY-ONE: "TIMESCAPE"

Written by Brannon Braga
Directed by Adam Nimoy

The original STAR TREK blooper reel includes a scene from 1966 when a 10 year old boy wearing pointed ears walked onto the bridge and called Mr. Spock, "daddy." That child was Leonard Nimoy's son, Adam. Twenty-seven years later, Adam Nimoy, an entertainment attorney turned director, is at the helm of "Timescape," one of the more challenging episodes of the sixth season.

Time travel has been explored in various ways on THE NEXT GENERATION. "Yesterdays Enterprise" altered time throughout the galaxy. The fifth season's "Cause And Effect" caught the Enterprise in a time loop. "Timescape" destroyed the Enterprise in a different manner.

This time the Enterprise and a Romulan ship are frozen in time. Only Picard, Data, Geordi and Troi know how to rescue them. Picard, Troi and Geordi discover an interesting fragmentation effect in the shuttle. The Enterprise and a Romulan ship work together, following unfriendly encounters in "Face of the Enemy" and "The Next Phase." It keeps us guessing.

They walk around the Enterprise even though it is frozen in time by scientific doublespeak,. Time flips back and forth at one point as the Enterprise explodes only to move back to its pre-detonation state. Clever twists and surprises populate the episode. Even the shuttle craft trip to find the Enterprise includes unusual little things that make the story intriguing from the start.

Adam Nimoy is a good director, particularly considering the complicated requirements of the story. This suspenseful, imaginative episode keeps you guessing right up to the climax. It's quite an accomplishment and easily one of the best sixth season entries.

EPISODE ONE HUNDRED FIFTY-TWO: "DESCENT"

Written by Ronald D. Moore
From a story by Jeer Taylor
Guest Cast: Jim Norton, Stephen Hawking

The Enterprise reaches the Federation outpost on Ohniaka Three. An away team finds that the Borg murdered all 274 members of the outpost. The Borg then ambush the away team.

Beginning with season three, THE NEXT GENERATION ran cliffhangers at the end of each season. They keep viewers anxious throughout the summer waiting for the fall premiere. We expect the return of "Hugh," the Borg from the fifth season. Instead we get Lore, Data's "evil twin" last seen in the fourth season. He returns leading a contingent of Borg.

Data began acting strangely early in year six, suffering a recurring dream in "Birthright." He became angry during a fight with the Borg in "Descent," then tried to duplicate the experience to better understand the emotion. His explorations led to uniting with a splinter group of Borg, currently led by Lore. The unexpected twist promised interesting developments in the seventh season.

SEASON

SEVEN

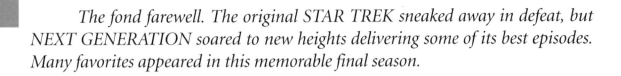

The fond farewell. The original STAR TREK sneaked away in defeat, but NEXT GENERATION soared to new heights delivering some of its best episodes. Many favorites appeared in this memorable final season.

SEASON SEVEN

EPISODE ONE HUNDRED FIFTY-THREE: "DESCENT II"

Written by Rene Echevarria
Directed by Alexander Singer
Guest Cast: Jim Norton, Stephen Hawking

Lore brings Data under control, leading the Borg against the Federation. A splinter group led by "Hugh" opposes him.

Hugh's individuality infected the Borg collective, disrupting it. Lore gave them new purpose, exterminating intelligent humanoids.

When Lore last appeared in "Brothers," he acquired the emotion chip intended for Data. It played havoc with Lore. Apparently he overcame that difficulty.

This slow moving episode is too talky. Lore seems in no hurry to use the Borg to conquer other worlds. Scene follows scene showing Geordi being tortured, Data threatening former friends and the plot to end Lore's control over Data. Hugh and his band of Borg revolutionaries are thrown into the mix. By the end it all seems anti-climactic.

They saved money by using few sets, but the biggest problem is the weak script. It limps to its inevitable resolution without surprises.

Parts of "Descent II" are riveting, but the whole is not as great as the sum of its parts. TNG seemed to have licked the problem of strong first parts and weak conclusions until this two-parter. Disappointing conclusions, with the exception of "Unification II," appear when they are the premiere episode of a season. It was a discouraging kick off for the final season.

EPISODE ONE HUNDRED FIFTY-FOUR: "LIAISONS"

Written by Jeanne Carrigan Fauci & Lisa Rich
Story by Roger Eschbacher & Jaq Greenspan
Directed by Cliff Bole
Guest Cast: Barbara Williams

Picard's shuttle crash-lands on a planetoid. A resident woman turns out to be more than she seems, and may be dangerous.

Season seven contains no real bombs but some episodes are quickly forgotten. This odd entry is one of them. It might more aptly be called mind games. Aliens test humans to better understand the human race. It's a padded story.

EPISODE ONE HUNDRED FIFTY-FIVE: "INTERFACE"

Written by Joe Menosky
Directed by Robert Wiemer
Guest Cast: Madge Sinclair, Ben Vareen

Geordi uses a virtual reality probe on a disabled vessel. He meets an entity that claims to be his mother.

The Virtual Reality probe device makes this a remarkable story. Geordi employs it to explore areas too dangerous for a person. The episode introduces his parents, and immediately kills off his mother. Geordi rarely gets character episodes. It is sad this story didn't serve him better.

Some things remain unexplained in the story, such as how the V.R. probe works. We always see Geordi walking around inside the distant craft. Is he supposed to be a hologram or what? It's not convincing when we're told Geordi is in danger when he's really safe back on the Enterprise wearing the V.R. suit.

Ben Vareen plays Geordi's father, Dr. LaForge, while Madge Sinclair plays his mother, Silva LaForge.

This episode has no subplot. It could have used one. The story is slow and drawn out.

EPISODE ONE HUNDRED FIFTY-SIX: "GAMBIT I"

Written by Naren Shankar
Story by Christopher Hatton and Naren Shankar
Directed by Alexander Singer
Guest Cast: Robin Curtis, Richard Lynch

A disguised Riker searches for the missing Captain Picard. Evidence shows that Jean-Luc is dead. That's how the episode begins.

We know he can't be dead, but it's an interesting way to start a story. There's no tedious set-up.

Picard turns up half-way through the episode, masquerading as a mercenary named Galen. It's the name of Picard's late archeology professor. He's on a pirate vessel with a varied crew, including a Vulcan. This is the first Vulcan criminal in STAR TREK. They plunder Romulan archeological sites, searching for an unspecified item.

Riker is captured by the mercenaries. Picard keeps him alive when the others want to kill him.

This part works well. The end, with the Enterprise being fired on, is an unimaginative cliffhanger. This interesting story is better than "Descent" or "All Good Things," a two hour episode destined to become a two-parter.

Interest arises from disparate characters on the mercenary ship. One is played by Robin Curtis, last seen in the beginning of STAR TREK IV: THE VOYAGE HOME. She plays a Romulan who turns out to be a Vulcan.

EPISODE ONE HUNDRED FIFTY-SEVEN: "GAMBIT II"

Written by Naren Shankar
Story by Christopher Hatton and Naren Shankar
Directed by Alexander Singer
Guest Cast: Robin Curtis, Richard Lynch

The Enterprise defeats the mercenaries, but they escape. "Galen" taunts Riker, who pretends to be angry over betraying his comrades. Picard uses his archeological skills on this mission to determine the right pieces, although he doesn't know the significance of the find.

Baran begins to trust Riker more than Galen. He wants Riker to kill Galen after they complete their mission. Picard jokes about this with Will, telling him, "You always seem to be after my job."

Interesting intrigue leads to the recreation of an ancient Vulcan weapon. The weapon has a logical underlying principle. It is the only NEXT GENERATION episode that reveals something new about Vulcan history.

This solid story possesses many interesting aspects, including its location on a vessel other than the Enterprise. Setting is important to story.

EPISODE ONE HUNDRED FIFTY-EIGHT: "PHANTASMS"

Written by Brannon Braga
Directed by Patrick Stewart

This mystery includes enough bizarre dream imagery to give viewers restless nights. In one instance, Deanna Troi appears as a living cake with pieces being cut from it.

Some fans weren't intrigued by this Data episode because it takes place in dreamland. Bizarre imagery supposedly communicates information to Data. It doesn't hold up to repeated viewing. Once you know the secret, the build-up becomes far less interesting.

It certainly contains weird events. Data opens his chest to answer an old-style telephone, and Deanna Troi turns into a cake.

The seventh season took chances. While not everyone viewed the experiments as successes, they were risks worth taking.

EPISODE ONE HUNDRED FIFTY-NINE: "DARK PAGE"

Written by Hillary J. Bader
Directed by Les Landau
Guest Cast: Majel Barrett

Lwaxana goes into a coma. Troi must enter her mother's mind and learn a terrible secret.

This episode offers the first dramatic turn for Lwaxana in a NEXT GENERATION episode since the fourth season's "Half A Life." The excellent story involves suppressed memories of a sister Deanna never knew she had. Lwaxana is portrayed as a fully dimensional character rather than just a cartoon as she was in "Haven" and other episodes.

Lwaxana plays a pivotal character, but it's a Troi episode. She isn't cut out as she was in past Lwaxana stories. There's enough melodrama to go around.

EPISODE ONE HUNDRED SIXTY: "ATTACHED"

Written by Naren Shankar
Story by Nicholas Sagan
Directed by Jonathan Frakes
Guest Cast: Robin Gammell, Lenore Kasdorf

A warring faction kidnaps Picard and Crusher. The paranoid culture believes that others are out to get them. They won't trust anyone. They're dishonest and assume everyone else is the same.

The captors telepathically link Picard and Crusher. They escape with the help of a member of the underground. During their flight to freedom, the telepathic link reveals subconscious desires for each other. The first signs of mutual attraction appeared in the first season. It was dropped until this episode.

Beverly and Jean-Luc look right together. It's surprising that their mutual attraction was not pursued during the previous six seasons. It's as if the writers forgot after year one and remembered in year seven. Nothing is hinted at in the movie STAR TREK: GENERATIONS. When Picard meets his fantasy family in the Nexus, his wife is not Beverly Crusher.

EPISODE ONE HUNDRED SIXTY-ONE: "FORCE OF NATURE"

Written by Naren Shankar
Directed by Robert Lederman
Guest Cast: Michael Corbett, Margaret Reed, Lee Arenberg

Alien scientists insist that warp drive engines endanger their corridor in space. The brother and sister team of scientists appear fanatic until their claims prove true. In subsequent episodes, only low warp speeds are allowed in some regions of space. Special permission must be obtained from Starfleet to exceed those restrictions.

Who suspected that the warp drive would become a political issue? This story logically reveals how it happens.

Spectacular special effects make it look as if they cut corners on other episodes to splurge on this one. The good story has a surprising and explosive climax.

EPISODE ONE HUNDRED SIXTY-TWO: "INHERITANCE"

Written by Dan Koeppel and Rene Echevarria
Story by Dan Koeppel
Directed by Robert Sheerer
Guest Cast: Fionnula Flanagan

Data meets the woman who assisted Dr. Noonian Soong in his creation. She is more than she seems.

More Data episodes appeared as he became more popular. This is the third in season seven. It presents the key to Data for the entire seven year run of NEXT GENERATION. The android meets his mother, Juliana Tainer. She harbors a secret she doesn't know she possesses.

Juliana is also an android, but doesn't know it. A message left in her for Data reveals that she nearly died. Dr. Soong saved her by transferring her consciousness into an android body. It is programmed to age naturally and finally die of old age.

It begs the question. Would Juliana choose to die?

Another issue is that Juliana is married. Her husband doesn't know that his wife is a machine. The episode never confronts this issue.

Since these are two normal married persons, it can be assumed that they enjoy normal marital relations. How would he feel after learning he has had sex with an android?

It may be that Gene Roddenberry's postulate has been applied. In the future all consenting sexual relations will be tolerated.

This is an excellent episode. Just when we thought there was nothing more to learn about Data's past, they reveal exciting new details.

EPISODE ONE HUNDRED SIXTY-THREE: "PARALLELS"

Written by Brannon Braga
Directed by Robert Wiemer

Worf returns to the Enterprise from a Klingon tournament. He finds things changed. They keep changing, particularly when he meets his wife, Deanna Troi.

It was the single most popular episode in the final season of NEXT GENERATION. The Worf episode involved the rest of the crew in crucial scenes. NEXT GENERATION explored alternate realities in exciting ways comparable to the original STAR TREK's "Mirror, Mirror." "Parallels" is even better. Worf shifts through a series of parallel universes, causing parallel Worfs to shift as well.

The climax reveals something of these other universes, including one in which the Borg have conquered the Federation. It is mind-bending.

A parallel universe was established in "Mirror, Mirror," and recently revisited on DEEP SPACE NINE. Thousands of parallel universes is something much more. The episode explores interesting aspects, such as Worf discovering that in one universe Picard wasn't rescued from the Borg. There's a touching scene when this Enterprise contacts Worf's Enterprise and Riker sees his old friend Jean-Luc alive and well.

This story shows fantastic, far-reaching possibilities.

EPISODE ONE HUNDRED SIXTY-FOUR: "THE PEGASUS"

Written by Ronald D. Moore
Directed by LeVar Burton
Guest Cast: Terry O'Quinn

Admiral Pressman arrives on board the Enterprise. Riker and his old commander no longer see eye to eye, particularly about a dangerous shared secret.

"The Pegasus" is as exciting as "Parallels." It explores the past of Commander Riker in a way that changes the Federation. The Romulans appear in this episode along with fabulous special effects. This wonderful mystery story delivers a satisfying payoff.

The story tells of a hunt and a mystery. The Enterprise hunts for the Pegasus, but we don't know why. A newly graduated Riker had been posted to the Pegasus. The well-trained junior officer stood by his captain against a mutiny. Looking back, Riker regrets that decision and now believes that the mutineers were right.

The Enterprise uncovers a conspiracy at a very high level of Starfleet. Picard blows the whistle. He also reveals the secret to the Romulans. Such a potentially disastrous political revelation is not within Jean-Luc's purview as a Starfleet Captain. Those who weren't conspirators but agreed with them would be angry with Picard. This is "career suicide." Jean-Luc would have faced early retirement or a post where he couldn't cause further problems.

The story leaves much to think about.

EPISODE ONE HUNDRED SIXTY-FIVE: "HOMEWARD"

Written by Naren Shankar
Story by Spike Steingasser
Directed by Alexander Singer
Guest Cast: Paul Sorvino

This episode reveals the dark side of the Federation. The Prime Directive dictates that the last survivors of a race of intelligent people on a doomed planet must die. Worf's foster brother intervenes and saves them.

Captain Picard supports the Federation decision. He seems to be a heartless martinet. Picard loses the respect his character gained over the seven seasons. Considering Picard's willingness to challenge Starfleet in "Pegasus," watching him turn his back on helpless people smacks of supporting genocide.

A character criticized the Federation for hiding behind the Prime Directive in the third season episode "The High Ground." "Homeward" proves the truth of that accusation!

Worf's previously unknown foster-brother beams the people into a holodeck representation of their cavern. They will be led to another land, actually another planet. The people will never know they were on a space craft, thereby upholding the spirit of the Prime Directive. That difficulties arise goes without saying, but it is worth the effort.

Worf, a Klingon, has as many relatives as all the other main characters combined. Over seven seasons we've met Worf's foster parents, foster-brother, son and Klingon brother. We've only met Geordi's parents, Riker's father, Picard's brother and nephew and Troi's mother. Worf's son, Alexander, is a semi-regular. He features in the most family sagas.

EPISODE ONE HUNDRED SIXTY-SIX: "SUB ROSA"

Written by Brannon Braga
Story by Jeri Taylor
Directed by Jonathan Frakes
Guest Cast: Shay Duffin, Duncan Regehr

Dr. Crusher buries her grandmother on the Caldos Colony. She encounters a family ghost. The episode hinges on Dr. Crusher's belief ghosts don't exist. The life form needs a willing human host to exist.

Beverly's mother died when Beverly was very young. She was then raised by her grandmother, also a doctor.

The Caldos Colony world was an early terraforming experiment, modeled after Scotland. Weather control prevents severe storms, unless a certain spirit interferes.

This rare NEXT GENERATION episode highlights sexuality. Ronin, the supposed ancient spirit, merges with women of Beverly's family, the Howards, granting them erotic experiences. Ronin has been the lover of Howard women for 800 years. He was the lover of Beverly's grandmother for many years.

Beverly finally decides Ronin is not a ghost or spirit, but an energy life form that needs a human host. Howard women possess a unique chemical property that allows the life form to merge with them.

The ordinarily benevolent entity kills a man. It seems contrived to justify what Beverly does at the end. Her grandmother's journal reveals a kind lover with no negative side effects of their parasite-host relationship. The parasite gave the women very intense orgasms. Beverly made a mistake at the end.

People who read THE WITCHING HOUR by Anne Rice think this episode bears remarkable resemblance.

EPISODE ONE HUNDRED SIXTY-SEVEN: "LOWER DECKS"

Written by Rene Echevarria
Story by Ronald Wilkerson and Jean Louise Matthias
Directed by Gabrielle Beaumont
Guest Cast: Shannon Fill, Patti Yasutake, Dan Gauthier, Alexander Enberg, Bruce Beatty

Junior officers are tested during a secret mission near the Cardassian demilitarized zone. The episode introduces several new characters in an intriguing story. It effectively involves the viewer in the lives of the new crew men. The story focuses on them to the virtual exclusion of the regulars.

This story brings a character back from "The First Duty." She's a Bajoran, although she might not have been in "The First Duty." That race had already been introduced by that time. She was one of Wesley Crusher's co-conspirators. When she is posted to the Enterprise, Captain Picard gives her a much harder time than he gave Wesley.

The story includes a secret mission to Cardassian space, intrigue and heroism in a well written and moving adventure.

EPISODE ONE HUNDRED SIXTY-EIGHT: "THINE OWN SELF"

Written by Ronald D. Moore
Story by Christopher Hatton
Directed by Winrich Kolbe

Data gets amnesia. Problems follow when he enters a primitive village slowly being poisoned by radioactivity. Data brought the radioactive metal into the village. He doesn't recognize the menace in his addled state. The writers use a cliche to craft a good story.

Data gets along well with children, perhaps due to his innocence. Now he befriends a little girl. He interacts with the pre-industrial culture, causing nearly lethal trouble, then correcting it. This is exactly what the Prime Directive prohibits.

Data is impaled on a pike in a surprising death scene. He's even buried. The Enterprise retrieves his body in its own inimitable fashion.

The "B" story is equally interesting. Deanna Troi takes her test for command rank. She refers to events in a past episode, "Disaster," when she explains why she wants to advance. She succeeds at a high personal cost. It is a good subplot with a sensible resolution

EPISODE ONE HUNDRED SIXTY-NINE: "MASKS"

Written by Joe Menosky
Directed by Robert Wiemer

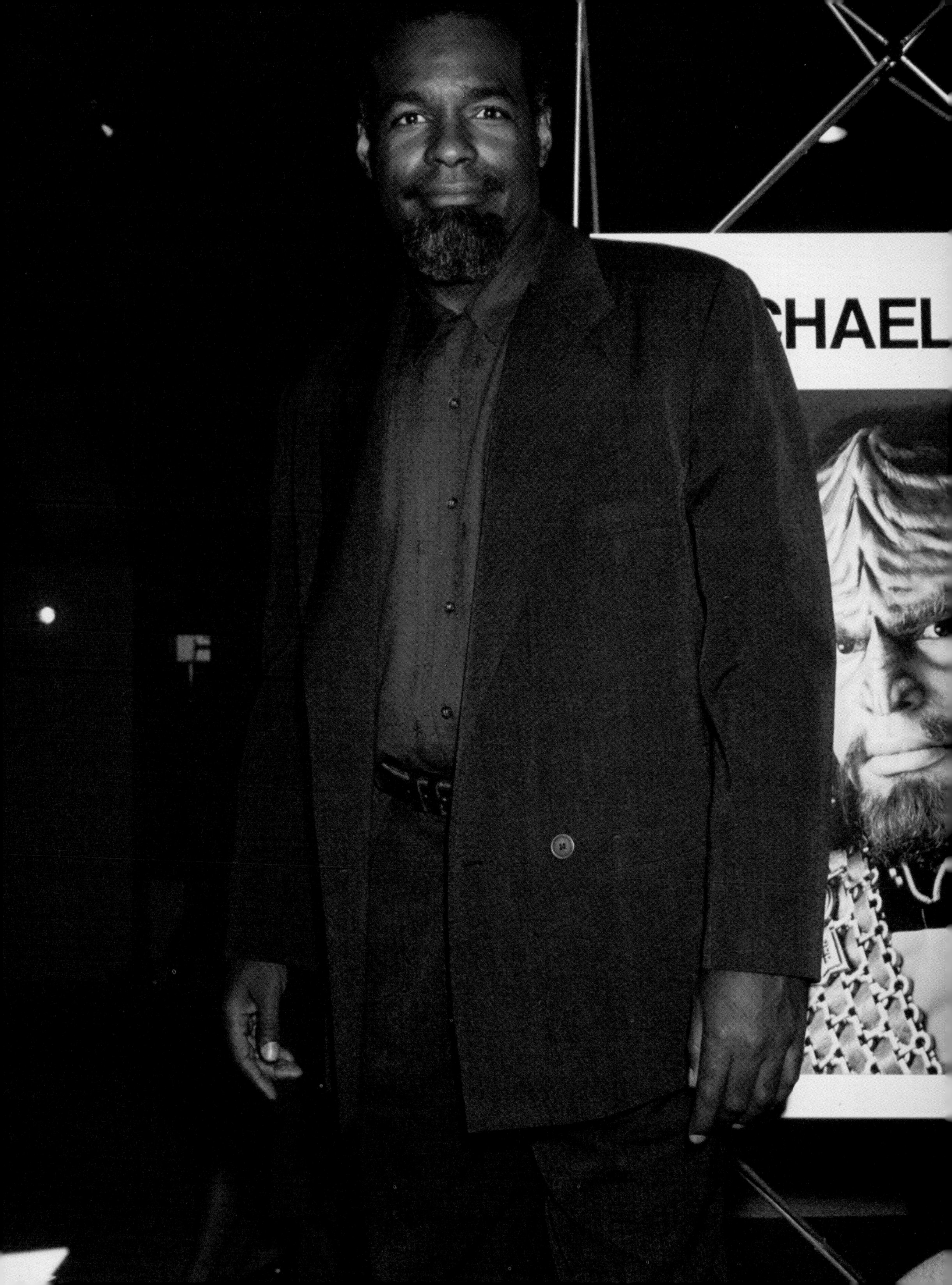
CHAEL

The Enterprise encounters a strange alien archive. It is drawn into the ship. The ship, including Data, begins to change into an ancient artifact.

The seventh season included weird episodes. This was one of them. The archive "infects" the Enterprise, transforming it into an alien Egyptian-like monument. Data changes in odd new ways.

The first clue something is really wrong comes when Geordi opens a photon torpedo casing and finds snakes. Things get stranger and stranger until an ancient being possesses Data. He wears a mask and looks like an ancient astronaut. The strange story makes you wonder.

EPISODE ONE HUNDRED SEVENTY: "EYE OF THE BEHOLDER"
Written by Rene Echevarria
Story by Brannon Braga
Directed by Cliff Bole

The suicide of a crew member leads to the unraveling of a mystery from the original construction of the Enterprise. The viewer thinks someone is killing people on the Enterprise to cover up a crime. It's a much stranger explanation than that.

When it ends, you discover much was a protracted dream sequence. You have to watch a second time to separate dream from reality. Part of the story shows Worf and Troi beginning a relationship as suggested in "Parallels."

The suicide at the beginning is shocking. A crew member hurls himself into an energy beam and is vaporized. The script creates a sense of loss for the unknown crewman and the incredulity his friends feel over the inexplicable death.

EPISODE ONE HUNDRED SEVENTY-ONE: "GENESIS"
Written by Brannon Braga
Directed by Gates McFadden

A cell infects the crew of the Enterprise. It transforms them into a variety of bizarre manifestations. Worf becomes a crab monster while Reginald Barclay turns into a giant spider. Picard and Data try to learn what caused the changes. The answer lies with Data's cat, Spot. She gives birth to kittens unaffected by the virus.

Bestial crew members hunt those unchanged. The demanding, nightmarish story challenged first time director Gates McFadden. Many in the cast wore heavy makeup.

This story appeared in the same season as "Masks." It forces a comparison. Both show wholesale transformations that have to be reversed aboard the Enterprise.

EPISODE ONE HUNDRED SEVENTY-TWO: "JOURNEY'S END"
Written by Ronald D. Moore

SEASON SEVEN

Directed by Corey Allen
Guest Cast: Wil Wheaton

Wesley Crusher returns in a story that ties together elements introduced in the first season. Wesley has graduated from Starfleet Academy. He no longer wants to be in Starfleet and opposes their plan to relocate a settlement of Native Americans from the Cardassian demilitarized zone.

The disgrace he suffered in "The First Duty" seems to have profoundly affected him. He's no longer the happy go lucky super jock he was in the Academy where he was considered one of the best of the upper classmen. Now he questions and actively opposes Starfleet actions. When violence breaks out, he turns and walks away!

The Traveler was introduced in "Where No One Has Gone Before." He appeared in another episode and then vanished until now. He returns to resolve events from the first season not pursued until now.

The episode brings an interesting resolution to ideas introduced nearly seven years ago. It also writes finis to a character Paramount chose not to include in the feature films.

EPISODE ONE HUNDRED SEVENTY-THREE: "FIRSTBORN"
Written by Rene Echevarria
Story by Mark Kalbfeld
Directed by Jonathan West
Guest Cast: Brian Bonsall

Worf and Alexander meet a mysterious stranger At a Klingon outpost. He changes both their lives. This Klingon episode involves Worf and Alexander. It rises above the usual nonsense.

The opening belies this. It begins with Alexander running into his quarters swiftly followed by a water balloon bursting against Worf's chest. The unexpected encounter leads to one of Worf's typically boring lectures. Alexander thinks his father is a spoil sport.

The story notes how difficult it is for Alexander to be the only Klingon growing up on the Enterprise. The isolation also affects Worf. When Worf lectures Alexander because he forgot something, he sounds like a dreary human parent.

Alexander announces that he doesn't want to undergo the first Age of Ascension ceremony. He doesn't want to be a warrior. By story's end we're uncertain whether he'll stick to this decision.

An interesting facet appears in this episode. Until this point Worf lectured Alexander about the directions his life should take, but by story's end Worf learns to accept what the future holds for his son. It may not be the traditional Klingon path.

Important episodes in this season mark turning points for Wesley Crusher, Ensign Ro and other characters. This episode marks an important turning point for Alexander.

EPISODE ONE HUNDRED SEVENTY-FOUR: "BLOODLINES"

Written by Nicholas Sagan
Directed by Les Landau
Guest Cast: Lee Arenberg, Ken Olandt

Daimon Bok first appeared in "The Battle," a first season episode. Picard's old Ferengi enemy returns and discovers that Jean-Luc has a long lost son. He threatens to kill the son because Picard killed Bok's son years before.

Picard searches for the son of a woman he had an affair with many years before. He believes it may be his son. Jean-Luc broke off the affair to remain in Starfleet. She may have been angry and not told him he had a son.

Touching scenes between Picard and the young man show a long lost father attempting to relate to a son he never knew existed. The son isn't sure he wants to know this stranger. The young man is something of a reprobate, although not a criminal. He's hardly the stuff that a starship captain would expect a son to be.

The climax reveals surprises. We again see how the Ferengi deal with one of their own who has forgotten that profit comes first, last and always.

EPISODE ONE HUNDRED SEVENTY-FIVE: "EMERGENCE"

Written by Joe Menosky
Story by Brannon Braga
Directed by Cliff Bole

The Enterprise acts on its own, doing strange, inexplicable things. They are all connected to the holodeck, which has developed a mind of its own. An emergent intelligence has merged with the Enterprise and is now reproducing.

Strange things happen in this episode. They lead to an inexplicable outcome. A train on the holodeck provides a metaphor for the curious events. The ending is anti-climactic. The explanation reminds me of an episode of SPACE: 1999 when a disembodied alien entity invaded the moon base, and then left everyone to wonder what it was all about. I had the same feeling at the end of this episode.

EPISODE ONE HUNDRED SEVENTY-SIX: "PREEMPTIVE STRIKE"

Written by Rene Echevarria
Story by Naren Shankar
Directed by Patrick Stewart
Guest Cast: Michelle Forbes

The Maquis, a group of anti-Cardassian terrorists introduced on DEEP SPACE NINE, figure prominently in one of the best episodes of season seven. This episode also features the long awaited return of Ensign Ro, an important regular during the fifth season. Ro Laren goes undercover to help the Federation destroy the Maquis and prevent a border war with the Cardassians. Ro discovers that the Maquis may be fighting the good fight after all.

Ro Laren provided a breath of fresh air when she was introduced in season five. She remains one of the most interesting regulars in any STAR TREK. Human characters are portrayed as too "perfect." Ensign Ro wasn't saddled with this baggage.

Her anti-Cardassian background made it easy for the Maquis to accept her. While DEEP SPACE NINE portrays the Maquis as extremists, this episode depicts the Cardassians as extremists and terrorists. It presents the Maquis as honest, committed people determined to protect their friends and family in the Cardassian demilitarized zone.

Ro Laren watches a man die whom she cared for a great deal. We understand why she aligns with the Maquis and becomes a renegade from Starfleet. Ro Laren feels great anguish at her betrayal of the trust Jean-Luc placed in her. She is portrayed with greater dimension than the other NEXT GENERATION regulars.

This fine character episode offers good drama and opens a variety of possibilities for Ensign Ro on DEEP SPACE NINE.

EPISODE ONE HUNDRED SEVENTY-SEVEN AND ONE HUNDRED SEVENTY-EIGHT: "ALL GOOD THINGS"

Written by Ronald D. Moore and Brannon Braga
Directed by Winrich Kolbe

Jean-Luc encounters Q again and becomes unstuck in time. He moves back and forth through three time periods connected by the same menace. It must be conquered in each time and place simultaneously.

This two hour finale is not as compelling as "Preemptive Strike." The complex plot shows a possible future for the characters and the Federation. The fun story bores on repeated viewing, just as "Parallels" and "Preemptive Strike" do.

The strength of "All Good Things" lies in the use of time travel. Picard interacts with the same people in different times, including Tasha Yar. The future Data has several pet cats.

Subplots in the future include lingering enmity between Worf and Riker over the death of Deanna Troi, the collapse of the Klingon-Federation armistice and Picard marrying then divorcing Beverly Crusher. The story depicted only one possible future. It may not come to pass.

"All Good Things" marks the end of STAR TREK: THE NEXT GENERATION as a television series. The final scene shows the poker game. Jean-Luc plays for the first time. It was the last scene filmed for the episode, adding a very touching ending.

VOYAGER

SPECIAL

STAR TREK premiered in 1966. Twenty-one years later the first STAR TREK spin-off, STAR TREK—THE NEXT GENERATION, hit the TV screen. The unprecedented seven year success of THE NEXT GENERATION led to DEEP SPACE NINE, the third STAR TREK series.

VOYAGER:
THE FUTURE OF STAR TREK

The third spin-off from the original STAR TREK marks the first with no input from Gene Roddenberry. He died in 1991.

Some argue that DEEP SPACE NINE also had no Roddenberry involvement. The series was announced months after Roddenberry's death, with nary a rumor escaping before. This time there can be no question. This is STAR TREK without Roddenberry.

THE NEW CAPTAIN

This series premiered in January 1995. Rick Berman, Michael Piller and Jeri Taylor created and produce it. STAR TREK: VOYAGER began with a Starfleet vessel, The Voyager, pursuing a Maquis ship, the rebels introduced on DEEP SPACE NINE and also seen in the TNG episode "Preemptive Strike."

Both ships fall into an uncharted wormhole to emerge in a galaxy hundreds of light years from home. The crews join forces to find their way back, and explore the new quadrant of space. Many compare it to LOST IN SPACE, although Roddenberry's TV series EARTH II is more similar.

Jonathan Frakes and Marina Sirtis wanted to be on VOYAGER, but Paramount preferred to start with a new cast. They want the NEXT GENERATION regulars to appear in big screen outings. Paramount compromised by allowing Jonathan Frakes to appear on the third year DEEP SPACE NINE episode "Defiant" as Thomas Riker, the transporter duplicate of Will Riker.

Behind the scenes stories abounded during the start-up of DEEP SPACE NINE. They also accompanied the painful birth of STAR TREK: VOYAGER. The studio denied many rumors, but couldn't hide Genevieve Bujold's departure. The first actress cast as Captain Kathryn Janeway, the series lead, quit after two days. TV GUIDE said she was difficult to work with. When she quit, no one begged her to return.

Bujold released no public statement. Her agent refuses to comment on the incident.

VOYAGER began production before Bujold quit. Another actress had to be cast. It caused production delays. Kate Mulgrew soon filled the role. She had been one of the actresses originally considered for the part. Mulgrew was best known as the star of the short-lived 1979 series MRS. COLUMBO. In recent years she appeared on the soap opera RYAN'S HOPE and in

VOYAGER

the Billy Crystal movie THROW MOMMA FROM THE TRAIN. She was most recently seen in the film CAMP NOWHERE.

SUPPORTING PLAYERS

The cast also includes Doc Zimmerman, a hologram played by Robert Picardo. Considering the portrayal of holograms on THE NEXT GENERATION, this will not demote him to minor status on the show. Picardo previously appeared in major roles in numerous films and TV series, including THE HOWLING and CHINA BEACH. Doc becomes a hologram after he is killed in the premiere episode. Picardo knows he's going to be compared to Picard because of his bald pate.

A regular Vulcan character appears for the first time since the original STAR TREK. Tim Russ plays Tuvok, the first black Vulcan in STAR TREK. Russ recently appeared in the movie MR. SATURDAY NIGHT.

Ethan Phillips portrays Neelix, the handyman and cook. He appeared as a regular on the TV series BENSON and in the movie THE SHADOW. This character is more like Quark than a hero.

Kes, the Ocampa companion of Neelix, is played by Jennifer Lien, late of ANOTHER WORLD and PHENOM. Ocampas live a brief nine years.

Roxann Biggs-Dawson plays half-human, half-Klingon Chief Engineer B'Elanna Torres. She recently appeared in the direct-to-video film DARKMAN 2.

Robert Beltran, previously seen on MODELS, INC., plays Capt. Chakotay, a Maquis. He's a native American from the Federation colony presented in the NEXT GENERATION episode "Journey's End." He goes on vision quests with his pet timber wolf.

Robert Duncan McNeill portrays Starfleet Lieutenant Tom Paris. He hides a secret past. The actor was a regular on the soap opera ALL MY CHILDREN.

Ops-Communications Officer Harry Kim is played by Garrett Wang, who previously appeared in the film ANGRY CAFE.

FACING THE FUTURE

NEXT GENERATION veteran Winrich Kolbe directed the two-hour premiere, "The Caretaker." It includes a brief DEEP SPACE NINE cross-over and an appearance by Quark. The adventures then head far from home as VOYAGER attempts to repeat the original STAR TREK and introduce a new cast of characters who visit planets and meet aliens never before encountered.

Although set in the same 24th Century time line as NEXT GENERATION and DEEP SPACE NINE, storylines and characters from those two series won't effect this show.

Rumors abounded early in 1994 when a number of new, young characters appeared prominently in the NEXT GENERATION episode "Lower Decks." It was wide-

VOYAGER

ly believed they were members of the forthcoming cast of STAR TREK: VOYAGER. This turned out not to be true. They never appeared again.

The future is poised to be unveiled again, just as it was two years ago when DEEP SPACE NINE premiered. Will STAR TREK launch another stellar success? Only the ratings can tell.

THE MAN WHO CREATED STAR TREK: GENE RODDENBERRY
James Van Hise

The complete life story of the man who created STAR TREK, reveals the man and his work.

$14.95 in stores ONLY $12.95 to Couch Potato Catalog Customers
160 Pages
ISBN # 1-55698-318-2

TWENTY-FIFTH ANNIVERSARY TREK TRIBUTE
James Van Hise

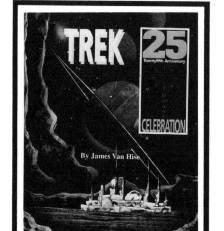

Taking a close up look at the amazing Star Trek stroy, this book traces the history of the show that has become an enduring legend. James Van Hise chronicles the series from 1966 to its cancellation in 1969, through the years when only the fans kept it alive, and on to its unprecedented revival. He offers a look at its latter-day blossoming into an animated series, a sequence of five movies (with a sixth in preparation) that has grossed over $700 million, and the offshoot "The Next Generation" TV series.

The author gives readers a tour of the memorials at the Smithsonian and the Movieland Wax Museums, lets them witness Leonard Nimoy get his star on the Hollywood Walk Of Fame in 1985, and takes them behind the scenes of the motion-picture series and TV's "The Next Generation." The concluding section examines the future of Star Trek beyond its 25th Anniversary.

$14.95.....196 Pages
ISBN # 1-55698-290-9

BATMANIA II
Written by James Van Hise

Available in June.
Updating BATMANIA to include coverage of the second movie plus additional new material.
$14.95
.Color cover,
black and white interior photos
ISBN#1-55698-315-8

BATMANIA
(3rd printing) Written by James Van Hise
Tracing the Batman phenomenon over the past 50 years, beginning with the character's creation by Bob Kane in 1939, and examining the changes in the pages of Detective Comics and his own title over the last five decades. Then the focus shifts to the two movie serials and jumps two decades to the enormously popular BATMAN television series of the 1960s, the primary focus of the book. Interviews with Adam West (Batman), Burt Ward (Robin), Yvonne Craig (Batgirl), Julie Newmar (The Catwoman), writer Stanley Ralph Ross and George Barris, who designed the various Bat-vehicles, bring the reader behind the scenes. Special sections showcase the innumerable collectibles inspired by the show, and the ongoing phenomenon that surrounds it.
BATMANIA is the ultimate Bat-book for Bat-fans!
$14.95..........164 pages Color Cover, Black and White Interior Photos
ISBN#1-55698-252-6

Couch Potato Inc.   5715 N. Balsam   Las Vegas, NV 89130   (702)658-2090

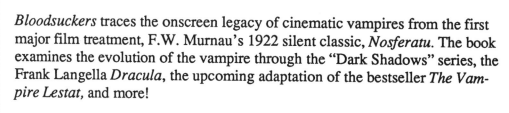

THE ADDAMS FAMILY REVEALED
James Van Hise

* One of the most popular series in television history recently released as a Major motion picture

Beginning with a detailed biography of Charles Addams, the creator of the panel cartoon that led to the television show, this book traces the entire story of Gomez, Morticia, and the rest of the happy crew from the earliest television episodes to the new feature film.

$14.95.....164 Pages
ISBN # 1-55698-300-X

BLOODSUCKER: Vampires at the Movies
Scott Nance

All the great neck-biters are here!

Bloodsuckers traces the onscreen legacy of cinematic vampires from the first major film treatment, F.W. Murnau's 1922 silent classic, *Nosferatu*. The book examines the evolution of the vampire through the "Dark Shadows" series, the Frank Langella *Dracula*, the upcoming adaptation of the bestseller *The Vampire Lestat,* and more!

$14.95.....160 Pages
ISBN # 1-55698-317-4

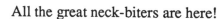

COUCH POTATO INC.   5715 N. Balsam Rd   Las Vegas, NV 89130   (702)658-2090

Use Your Credit Card 24 HRS — Order toll Free From: **(800)444-2524** Ext 67

BORING, BUT NECESSARY ORDERING INFORMATION

Payment:

Use our new 800 # and pay with your credit card or send check or money order directly to our address. All payments must be made in U.S. funds and please do not send cash.

Shipping:

We offer several methods of shipment. Sometimes a book can be delayed if we are temporarily out of stock. You should note whether you prefer us to ship the book as soon as available, send you a merchandise credit good for other goodies, or send your money back immediately.

Normal Post Office: $3.75 for the first book and $1.50 for each additional book. These orders are filled as quickly as possible. Shipments normally take 5 to 10 days, but allow up to 12 weeks for delivery.

Special UPS 2 Day Blue Label Service or Priority Mail: Special service is available for desperate Couch Potatoes. These books are shipped within 24 hours of when we receive the order and normally take 2 to 3 three days to get to you. The cost is $10.00 for the first book and $4.00 each additional book .

Overnight Rush Service: $20.00 for the first book and $10.00 each additional book.

U.s. Priority Mail: $6.00 for the first book and $3.00.each additional book.

Canada And Mexico: $5.00 for the first book and $3.00 each additional book.

Foreign: $6.00 for the first book and $3.00 each additional book.

Please list alternatives when available and please state if you would like a refund or for us to backorder an item if it is not in stock.

COUCH POTATO INC.   5715 N. Balsam Rd   Las Vegas, NV 89130   (702)658-2090

Use Your Credit Card 24 HRS — Order toll Free From: **(800)444-2524** Ext 67

ORDER FORM

_____ Trek Crew Book $9.95
_____ Best Of Enterprise Incidents $9.95
_____ Trek Fans Handbook $9.95
_____ Trek: The Next Generation $14.95
_____ The Man Who Created Star Trek: $12.95
_____ 25th Anniversary Trek Tribute $14.95
_____ History Of Trek $14.95
_____ The Man Between The Ears $14.95
_____ Trek: The Making Of The Movies $14.95
_____ Trek: The Lost Years $12.95
_____ Trek: The Unauthorized Next Generation $14.95
_____ New Trek Encyclopedia $19.95
_____ Making A Quantum Leap $14.95
_____ The Unofficial Tale Of Beauty And The Beast $14.95
_____ Complete Lost In Space $19.95
_____ ..doctor Who Encyclopedia: Baker $19.95
_____ Lost In Space Tribute Book $14.95
_____ Lost In Space With Irwin Allen $14.95
_____ Doctor Who: Baker Years $19.95
_____ Doctor Who: Pertwee Years $19.95
_____ Batmania Ii $14.95
_____ The Green Hornet $14.95 _____ Special Edition $16.95

_____ Number Six: The Prisoner Book $14.95
_____ Gerry Anderson: Supermarionation $17.95
_____ Addams Family Revealed $14.95
_____ Bloodsucker: Vampires At The Movies $14.95
_____ Dark Shadows Tribute $14.95
_____ Monsterland Fear Book $14.95
_____ The Films Of Elvis $14.95
_____ The Woody Allen Encyclopedia $14.95
_____ Paul Mccartney: 20 Years On His Own $9.95
_____ Yesterday: My Life With The Beatles $14.95
_____ Fab Films Of The Beatles $14.95
_____ 40 Years At Night: The Tonight Show $14.95
_____ Exposing Northern Exposure $14.95
_____ The La Lawbook $14.95
_____ Cheers: Where Everybody Knows Your Name $14.95
_____ SNL! The World Of Saturday Night Live $14.95
_____ The Rockford Phile $14.95
_____ Encyclopedia Of Cartoon Superstars $14.95
_____ How To Create Animation $14.95
_____ How To Draw Art For Comic Books $14.95
_____ King And Barker:an Illustrated Guide $14.95
_____ King And Barker: An Illustrated Guide II $14.95

100% Satisfaction Guaranteed.

We value your support. You will receive a full refund as long as the copy of the book you are not happy with is received back by us in reasonable condition. No questions asked, except we would like to know how we failed you. Refunds and credits are given as soon as we receive back the item you do not want.

NAME:_____

STREET:_____

CITY:_____

STATE:_____

ZIP:_____

TOTAL:_____ SHIPPING_____

SEND TO: Couch Potato, Inc. 5715 N. Balsam Rd., Las Vegas, NV 89130